P9-CFY-914

THICKER
than
WATER

THICKER
than
WATER

A Memoir

KERRY
WASHINGTON

Little, Brown Spark
New York   Boston   London

The stories in this book reflect the author's recollection of events. Some names, locations, and identifying characteristics have been changed to protect the privacy of those depicted. Dialogue has been re-created from memory.

Copyright © 2023 by Kerry Washington

Hachette Book Group supports the right to free expression and the value of copyright. The purpose of copyright is to encourage writers and artists to produce the creative works that enrich our culture.

The scanning, uploading, and distribution of this book without permission is a theft of the author's intellectual property. If you would like permission to use material from the book (other than for review purposes), please contact permissions@hbgusa.com. Thank you for your support of the author's rights.

Little, Brown Spark
Hachette Book Group
1290 Avenue of the Americas, New York, NY 10104
littlebrownspark.com

First Edition: September 2023

Little, Brown Spark is an imprint of Little, Brown and Company, a division of Hachette Book Group, Inc. The Little, Brown Spark name and logo are trademarks of Hachette Book Group, Inc.

The publisher is not responsible for websites (or their content) that are not owned by the publisher.

The Hachette Speakers Bureau provides a wide range of authors for speaking events. To find out more, go to hachettespeakersbureau.com or email hachettespeakers@hbgusa.com.

Little, Brown and Company books may be purchased in bulk for business, educational, or promotional use. For information, please contact your local bookseller or the Hachette Book Group Special Markets Department at special.markets@hbgusa.com.

Print book interior design by Bart Dawson

ISBN 9780316497398 (hardcover) / 9780316570510 (large print) / 9780316571777 (signed edition) / 9780316571760 (B&N signed edition) / 9780316571739 (B&N Black Friday signed edition)

Library of Congress Control Number: 2023935751

Printing 1, 2023

LSC-C

Printed in the United States of America

To my personal superheroes:
Chitterlin' Man and Hot Sauce;
Pump, Snacks, and Man-Man;
and to Babe

CONTENTS

THICKER
than
WATER

~∽∽~

This book is the result of my attempts to make sense of myself and my family and to accept the truth about who we are. I've written this account to more fully understand this truth, to affirm it, and to embrace it. This truth has given birth to a deeper compassion and love for my parents, and for myself. And I share it with you because I do not want to hide.

~∽∽~

PROLOGUE

got a text from my mother.

Where are you?

I quickly typed, **On my way home.**

I was sitting in my car at a stoplight at Coldwater Canyon and Ventura Boulevard in Sherman Oaks, just north of the city of Los Angeles.

Three rippling iPhone dots, then a reply:

We need to talk to you.

This was odd. Up to that point, my parents hadn't been people who dove headfirst into difficult conversations. The articulation of their "need" was striking. And the "we"—the presentation of themselves as a unified pair—was in some ways even more peculiar.

Today? I texted, wanting more details without asking the obvious question: *Why?*

Yes.

The day was Tuesday, April 3, 2018. To my right was a 76 gas station; to my left, a Ralphs supermarket. Behind me in the distance were my new offices at CBS Radford Studio Center, where my production company, Simpson Street (named after the street my mother grew up on in the Bronx), was developing a pilot episode of a new half-hour comedy (a show that would never see the light of day). It was a routine stop at a regular traffic intersection on a standard Southern California afternoon.

The morning had been productive, filled with meetings for our new pilot. There was a lot to accomplish before tape night: actors to be cast, contracts to sign, scripts to be refined, sets to be built. Being busy is one of the ways I create a sense of safety and control during times when I feel like there is none. This was one of those times. For many years leading up to this point I had been blessed with an acting job that was as close as an actor can get to stability and security. I was gifted with a lead role, *the* lead role, on a hit network television drama. In those years of steady employment, I had held the golden egg, but three weeks earlier, I'd finished filming my last-ever scenes on *Scandal*.

When we wrapped, it had felt like a revelatory gift in the truest sense. I had completed, in those seven seasons, a cycle of creative productivity that had changed not only my life, but the lives of hundreds of cast and crew members, and impacted millions of viewers around the world. It had been an exhilarating and exhausting ride. Aside from being a massive hit, it also had a profound cultural impact on several fronts. We were one of the first television productions to harness the burgeoning power of social media; we revolutionized the landscape of workplace fashion; we portrayed women as a central part of the democratic process; we were the first show to portray an abortion procedure on-screen; and we'd proved that a woman of color could lead a primetime network drama, something that hadn't been done in my lifetime.

But all that was behind me now. Today, I was filled with the pleasure of being busy. Our new TV show was something that could not possibly have been any more different from *Scandal*— a half-hour, multiple-camera situation comedy filmed in the Valley, on the other side of the Santa Monica Mountains, miles from the center of Hollywood, where *Scandal* had been born.

Before my mother's text arrived, as I sat in my car, my heart had been full of joyful possibilities. In the short term, I was heading home to meet up with family. My cousin John; his wife, Milly; and their three children were visiting from the East Coast to spend spring break with my husband and me and our three children. There were plans that afternoon for all of us to go to an interactive art exhibit called Candytopia.

In the longer term, a shift had occurred in my life. Now that the draining intensity of *Scandal* was over, I felt unmoored. I was heeding a deep call to adventure, one filled with a new set of unknowns.

I reread my mother's text. **We need to talk to you.**

What's wrong? What's happening? What do they need?

I began to tap into a mode of hypervigilance that had become one of my vital tools for survival. None of this was normal. We were not a family that made special time to "talk" unless something was wrong. Those conversations were few and far between. And when the accommodations to talk had been made, it was never good news.

When the light changed, I turned left to head up the canyon and called my husband, Nnamdi. I repeated the text exchange to him.

"That's so strange, right?"

"What do you think is going on?" he asked.

"I don't know," I said, "but I can't imagine it's good. Maybe someone is sick? Maybe it's something with the law?"

There had been tough conversations between my parents and me on both of those difficult subjects in the past, conversations that had led to them reluctantly revealing painful family secrets that they had kept from me in their effort to love and protect me as best they could. I couldn't help but wonder if this was another chapter of truth waiting to unfold. It was impossible to know for sure, given the limited intelligence that had been conveyed in those texts. Somewhere in my psyche I already knew that it was not good news, but I had made up my mind to wade in.

"I'm going to head to the apartment," I said to Nnamdi. At the next light I texted my mother the same and made the decision to head back east, toward whatever talk awaited me.

~~~

"The apartment" was a two-bedroom condo in a doorman building in West Hollywood. I'd bought it when Nnamdi and I were dating but not yet engaged. Before filming the pilot for

Scandal, I had moved back to New York; but when the show was in full swing, it was clear that I was becoming a California resident, and I'd needed to find a more permanent place to live. We had not yet gotten to the point in our relationship where it felt right to buy a home together, so asserting my fierce independence, I resolved to secure a place of my own. Years later, once we were married and had moved into our house in the Hollywood Hills, the apartment became the perfect landing spot for when my New York–based parents came to visit for more extended periods of time, something they started to do after the arrival of our daughter, Isabelle.

It took about half an hour to reach the apartment, on winding roads through Coldwater Canyon and Mulholland and Laurel Canyon, roads that often intimidate drivers who are new to LA. But I learned to drive on roads like this, twisting and turning my way through summers in the Catskill Mountains in upstate New York, where, as a teenager, I learned the limits of my "fierce independence" when my rejection of my mother's gentle directives caused me to sideswipe a parked car.

There had been no more text exchanges since I'd told my mom I was on my way. When I arrived at the apartment, I parked in the basement and pressed the button to call the elevator. So much change had unfolded while living in this building, so much life had been lived there. Date nights, labor pains, birthdays, couture fittings, *Scandal* rehearsals, *Game of Thrones* watch parties, baby's first solid foods, and first steps. As I stepped onto the elevator, I wondered what new memories today's conversation would etch into my heart. The closer I traveled toward my parents, with each passing floor, the more clearly I felt the weight of their request to speak.

The elevator door rattled open on the ninth floor. And as I turned left to face the precipice, my heart began to race. Light seeped from under the large wooden doors, and I was struck by the cavernous silence on the other side of them. I took a deep breath, readying myself for whatever revelations awaited me, and knocked. My mother's footsteps approached with a steady pace along the hardwood floor. The dense sound of the lock sliding open echoed in the empty hallway.

She opened the door, looked at me, and smiled in her slightly distant way, but today there was an extra measure of sadness in her eyes. As she turned to walk ahead of me into the living room, I could see my dad, silhouetted by the bright sunlight that streamed through the floor-to-ceiling windows at the back of the apartment.

We were all there, our family of three: Earl, Valerie, and Kerry. Father, mother, and only child. The Washingtons. But the room felt empty, somehow; incomplete. There wasn't a ton of furniture, just two armchairs and a couch. There had once been a large ottoman in the center of the room, but Nnamdi and I had recently taken it to our house to replace a dangerous, sharp-edged coffee table that had proved too difficult to baby-proof for our toddler son. I looked around and thought that perhaps I should be taking better care of my parents, providing them with more elaborate comforts and décor.

"Hey guys," I said, casually, wanting to convey that I was ready and able to metabolize whatever it was that they "needed" to share with me.

I sat down in the armchair closest to the door, my back to the entryway. My mother sat across from me, and my dad folded himself into the corner of the couch, as far from me as possible. No one said anything.

I wanted to try to make this as easy for them as I could. I already knew that for the past few weeks, my dad had been having sleepless nights and panic attacks.

Neither of them could look at me. Or at each other.

"Hey guys," I said again, and then, attempting to open a pathway into the discussion, I offered, "So, what's going on?"

In the silence, I looked around, searching the room for clues. There were many things that I cherished about that apartment, but at the top of the list was the view. The balcony that sat behind my parents provided an extraordinary south-facing perspective of Los Angeles. On a clear day you could see from the skyscrapers of downtown all the way to the Pacific. But even seated as I was, in the blue armchair that cradled me, I could see, behind my mother, endless skies with whispery white clouds hanging daintily in the blue, waiting for our conversation to take flight.

My mother took a deep breath, looked down, then up at me, and then down again—at her hands this time. Then back to me.

And then she started to speak.

"Forty-three years ago, we were having a really hard time having a child...."

Everything slowed. My body felt suddenly heavy. My eyes started to burn as a kind of haze crept across them. The sound of my own breathing almost drowned out my mother's words, but, as if underwater, I strained my ears to listen, finally, to the truth.

CHAPTER ONE

UNITED

"What will you do instead?"

It was late on a February morning in 2018, at Sunset Gower Studios in Hollywood, California. I was standing on a bare wooden platform behind the wall of a fake Truman Balcony. And it was Bellamy Young who had just asked that question—or rather, her character, Mellie Grant.

Emotions were running high. This would be the last scene of *Scandal* that Bellamy and I would share after arcing through seven seasons of emotional complexity as our characters Olivia Pope and Mellie Grant journeyed from enemies to allies, and then to partners, and finally, to friends. And in real life, during that time, Bellamy and I had come to share a sense of sisterhood that neither of us could have predicted. In the earliest days of *Scandal*, Bellamy's character, Mellie, was only a small supporting role on the show. Bellamy was originally cast to be a "day player." Day players are actors who are cast in a role in which their work can be completed in one day. In our pilot episode (which took, in total, ten days to film), Bellamy had just three lines, one of which was simply to proclaim my character's nickname, "Liiiiiiiiiv!" as she welcomed me into a quiet corner of a pretend Camp David.

By the end of the first season of *Scandal*, it was clear that Bellamy Young was a force to be reckoned with, and her character was a vital element in the magic alchemy that made *Scandal* a success. By the end of the series, Bellamy and our team of writers, led by Shonda Rhimes, our brilliant showrunner and titan of film and television, had transformed her character from the betrayed wife of a cheating president into the sitting president of the United States herself and a central character on *Scandal*.

Today's conversation on the balcony would be the last scene Bellamy would ever film during the life of our show, and it would be the last scene our entire production crew ever shot on our version of the Truman Balcony.

Not all our time working on the Truman Balcony had been fun. The scenes filmed there were some of our toughest and most time-consuming to complete. The entire exterior landscape outside the White House was created with advanced CGI technology, which meant that our construction of the balcony, and the platforms surrounding it, were enveloped in walls of blue screen that ran twenty feet high and one hundred and fifty feet wide. What replaced those blue screens in post-production were images called plates, which had been taken from the actual White House balcony. This had never been done before.

Many shows and films had created what they imagined to be the view from that balcony, but *Scandal* had been able to film actual footage from the balcony and then use those images. This remarkable access had been possible because of Shonda's strong relationship with the Obamas, and permission to film these plates had been granted when she'd paid a visit to the residence.

Most times, when I stared out onto the blue screen, as I was doing that morning, I thought of my own time on the real Truman Balcony. Years before, following a photo shoot for a shared cover of *Glamour* magazine with Michelle Obama and Sarah Jessica Parker, the First Lady invited us for lunch just inside the balcony. At that lunch, in that secluded haven, we'd spent time reflecting on the loss of anonymity and privacy—neither mine nor Sarah's as dramatic as the First Lady's. And I witnessed Michelle Obama's reverence for this little patch of elevated outdoor space that allowed her some sense of freedom within her cloistered existence. Now, as I prepared to complete this final scene with Bellamy, I thought about all the amazing places that my political life—both real and imaginary—had taken me.

In the years leading up to this scene, the pretend balcony had witnessed Olivia Pope in love, in anger, in pain, in joy, wielding power, feeling powerless . . . but this was the end. After we finished this scene, the entire Truman Balcony set would be ripped apart and destroyed. And although I knew that this set, these characters, and these circumstances in the script were not real, I discovered so much about this moment that felt like truth.

I had memorized the scene and practiced its possible rhythms alone in my head — and out loud with an assistant in the hair and makeup trailer — but when I actually heard the final question come out of Bellamy's mouth, "What will you do instead?" my heart leapt. For seven seasons I'd given the character of Olivia Pope and the show, our audiences, and our cast and crew, every available ounce of my soul. I had worked harder than I ever knew was possible and had sacrificed elements of my life that I had not been prepared for: my health, my privacy, any number of personal relationships.

Don't get me wrong: The rewards far outweighed the costs — my life and my career had been transformed. And I had been gifted with seemingly endless opportunities, responsibilities, commitments, and priorities. Which is partly why when I opened my mouth to answer the question, I was overwhelmed with joy and excitement, and I responded from the deepest truth of me. The words that had been scripted for Olivia Pope rose in me with the force of a thirty-foot wave.

"Whatever I want," I said.

And with that answer, both Olivia Pope and the actor playing her declared an approach to what felt like the beginnings of freedom. Olivia was no longer tethered by professional or personal obligations and expectations. And with *Scandal* coming to an end, neither was I. A weight was being lifted.

I had for my entire life felt an intense pressure to succeed, to get everything unendingly right. And of course, one of the things that I learned while playing Olivia Pope is that she did, too. But no more. I hoped we were both going to be free now. Released from the weight of what the world needed us to do and be.

We shot multiple takes that day—over and over I answered the line as it was written, "Whatever I want." It became almost a mantra, or a spell, or an intoxicating incantation. I was thrilled for Olivia Pope and for me. Together, we had done our work—we had made history and shifted the landscape of popular culture—and it was now time to be free.

At some point toward the end of the morning, we were in my close-up coverage. This is the moment when the camera is placed within its closest distance to the actor and uses the lens that captures the most intensely intimate view of them. I was delivering the line with all the joy that was surging through me. Our directing producer, Tom Verica, walked over to me. Tom is a brilliant director whose insights I always welcomed because the notes he gave usually led me toward my best performance of a scene.

"Hey," he whispered through his quiet smile, "can you try a version that is not quite as..." He took a careful breath and said, "*Happy?*"

And it hit me. Something was happening to Olivia Pope in that moment on that balcony. There was the obvious joy to feel and express about her future, for sure, but Olivia Pope and I were also saying goodbye. I looked at Bellamy and saw that she had tears in her eyes. I was not surprised. Bellamy is someone whose intellectual and emotional intelligence far exceeds mine. She needed no directive to grapple with the emotional truth of this goodbye; she was fully processing it all. But for me, the depth of this moment required more unfolding.

As I sat out there on that balcony, a realization slowly washed over me. In choosing now to be and do whatever felt most right to her, Olivia was admitting that up until that point she had mostly lived through, and for, other people. Olivia had never wholly done what she wanted—it wasn't even clear that she'd ever known exactly what that was. Freed from her father, and from her life as a fixer, Olivia was finally able to discover the truth of who she was without those defining forces.

My breathing deepened. What had initially felt like joy began to morph into grief. Bellamy and I were saying goodbye—to the show, to our characters, to each other, to who we had been in the world for these past seven seasons, and to the dedication that had been required of us to do so. The future stood in contrast to the sacrifices of the past, both personal and professional. And as it was now Olivia's time to do whatever she wanted and to be her most authentic self, perhaps it was time for me to do the same.

So, I thought, *do I even know who that authentic self is? If I am no longer Olivia Pope, who am I?*

In these years, I had become Olivia Pope, but I had also become "Kerry Washington," the star of this historic network drama. In a matter of days, both of these roles would be slipping away, and I would be left standing at the threshold of a new adventure.

~⌇~

When my parents began to date in the late sixties, they were not strangers to each other. My mother, Valerie Patricia Moss, went to high school with and befriended a kind young woman from Brooklyn named Claudell Washington. Claudell was bright and sweet and funny—easy to be with. But in the context of their lives up until that age, these young women might as well have been from separate universes. They had been raised on opposite sides of New York City and they came from very different families and ethnic cultures, but in each other they found a sisterhood that would last far longer than either could have imagined.

Both young women had been identified as "special and gifted" early in their schooling, and each had ventured beyond the boroughs of their births (my mother, the Bronx; Claudell, Brooklyn) to attend high school on the exciting and exotic island of Manhattan. Decades later I would be invited to make a similar pilgrimage from the Bronx to Manhattan, also in pursuit of a more challenging education.

Back in those days, though, each borough had been a world unto itself. So while they both attended Washington Irving High School, they had no exposure to each other's place of origin. There were no visits to each other's homes, no sleepovers, no shared family vacations.

What they *did* share were secrets and dreams and wishes, as well as the mundane realities of their family and personal lives. My mother worked as a home health aide and then later in the pet department at Macy's in Herald Square, and was one of seven children; Claudell was discouraged from working at all, and was one of two. Claudell's younger brother, Earl, was charming, brash, and cocky, and a bit of a track star in the competitive scene of high school athletics in New York City.

After graduation, my mother attended college on a beautiful campus in the Bronx that was then called Hunter Uptown and is today called Lehman College. Part of the City University of New York, Lehman College is also where, after many years of teaching in New York City Public Schools, my mother returned and began her career as a professor, eventually running the graduate program for elementary and early childhood education and both designing and implementing a groundbreaking program for teachers of color called the Teacher Opportunity Corps. It was while attending Hunter Uptown as a younger woman that my mother met her first husband, another student. The two soon married; however after a few tumultuous years, they divorced.

After the divorce, Claudell, with whom she had remained close, told my mother that she was attending a house party in the Bronx thrown by her cousin, Olive, who would later become my godmother. As the story goes, my dad—Claudell's younger brother, Earl—arrived at the party with a date, but he spent the whole evening talking to my mother on the back porch of the house on 216th Street and Barnes Avenue in the North Bronx. Given that my dad had just returned from a trip to the 1968 Mexico City Olympic Games, and my mother was headed to a vacation in that same city, there was lots to talk about.

My dad has attended three Olympic Games in his lifetime — the Games combine two of the things he loves most: sports and international culture. Earl's profile in high school athletics had led him to run for both the University of Pittsburgh and the US Army. He had been stationed in Germany, and it was there that his love for travel had been born. He spent all his free time adventuring through Europe, absorbing the various languages and cultures. That love had taken him to Mexico City, where he had witnessed Tommie Smith and John Carlos raise their fists on the podium to proclaim Black Power.

My parents' initial conversation lasted well into the wee hours of the morning, and my dad asked my mother what her plans were for the following afternoon, because he was going to the beach with some friends. He invited her to meet him, and they agreed to continue their conversation there.

The crew met up at Riis Beach in the Rockaways, on the southern tip of Queens. Having never seen a Black woman so fearlessly embrace the waves, my dad says that he fell in love with my mother the instant she dove into the ocean. It would be many more months before they started to date (neither remembers their first kiss), but my dad would later say that the image of my mother frolicking in the surf in a gorgeous two-piece was all the inspiration his heart required.

They swam together that day. And although they had known each other for over a decade — because of my mother's friendship with Claudell, they had often found themselves in the same room at the same time at the same weddings and christenings — in the water, in the frothy waves of the Atlantic on that afternoon, their shared existence as partners in life was born.

I think about that afternoon often, reflecting on what exactly it was about my mother's dive into the ocean that so entranced my dad. For sure it was her beauty — to this day, he tells me she looked incredible — but there was also something rebellious, courageous, adventurous, about that dive. Given the modern history of segregation in public pools, and the far-reaching history of trauma inflicted upon African Americans during the transatlantic slave trade, many of us carry a complicated and painful relationship with swimming in general, and swimming in the ocean in particular. What my dad saw that day was a woman willing to boldly break from convention. She was not like any other Black woman he had ever met, and, as he watched the stroke of her arms pull her through the water, he realized instantly that she was determined to carve her own path.

~~~

My mother and her six siblings were born to Clifford Mancle and Isabelle, Jamaicans who, like many immigrants to this country, came through Ellis Island in 1927 and 1929, respectively. Unlike many European immigrants, though, what they found in the United States was a complicated obstacle course of not only class, but caste.

Mancle and Isabelle hailed from the Parish of St. Elizabeth in the southwest corner of Jamaica. Despite his country of origin and his mixed heritage, Mancle looked like a northern European immigrant—fair-skinned with angular features. He was an alcoholic, but a jovial one—if he won money playing the numbers, he was the "spent it all before I got home" kind of drinker. He died when my mother was fifteen, leaving her and her siblings in the sole care of their mother. Like her husband, Isabelle was also from a mixed background, but her features told a more obvious story of the African and Arawak heritage that ran in both of their bloodlines. And unlike her jovial husband, there was a seriousness about Isabelle, a sense that she had been through a lot, was carrying multiple burdens, and was to be respected.

Due to growing up as both mixed race and a first-generation American, in many ways my mother's identity was born of the complexity of being othered. She was not raised within the cultural mores of American Blackness; she was the child of immigrants, a Caribbean kid, and accordingly had more in common with the other Caribbean children in school. While a few of my mother's sisters presented as, and identified with, other ethnic communities who seemed more racially ambiguous (Italian or Latine, for example), my mother was the darkest of her siblings and did not have the privilege of trying on different racial identities. Valerie Moss presented as Black, and she knew so from an early age.

In their home, as in many Caribbean households, a premium was placed on having lighter skin. Centuries of white supremacy and institutional racism led to internalized beliefs that the closer one's appearance aligned with European aesthetics, the more valued they were as human beings. My mother experienced the effects of this colorism firsthand. She was not the child chosen to represent the family on various outings or community events; her darker hue meant that she was not celebrated for her beauty.

Later in life my grandmother developed dementia, and as her faculties unraveled, so did her prejudices. The great irony was that my mother survived this coded racism within her family only to watch the matriarch of the family choose Michael Jordan, a tall, bald, handsome, dark-skinned man, to be her imaginary lover. Thanks to his repeated appearances as a spokesman for Ballpark Franks—"they plump when you cook 'em!"—my grandmother thought he was her boyfriend coming to visit her with lunch.

As she got older, notwithstanding her brown skin, the traits stemming from my mother's European roots—her thinner lips, more Anglican nose, less coarse hair—aligned her appearance with a beauty that was considered exotic. While in her Caribbean home her appearance was deemed "less than," in the larger Black community she was thought of as a beautiful oddity. The wounds inflicted in her youth run deep, however, and she spent most of her life feeling more odd than beautiful. My mother, believing that it was not an option to traffic on her looks or rely on the unconditional love of her family, was determined to be smart, independent, self-reliant, and successful. That determination, as well as the struggle with self-esteem that inspired it, was passed on to me.

~⌇~

My dad's mother's family was rooted in New York, with a lineage that we were told included the Shinnecock tribe of Long Island. My dad's father was born in Brooklyn and raised in Harlem, but before that "his people" hailed from the sea islands of South Carolina—Gullah Geechee country. Samuel Washington was a hardworking family man who adored his wife.

When I was in high school, my family went to St. Helena Island, off the coast of South Carolina, for the first time to visit our property—the land on the island had been handed down through my grandfather's family.

St. Helena Island is one of the Sea Islands off the coast of South Carolina, Georgia, and Florida. These islands were renowned as havens for African slaves who escaped plantations and created intact communities that upheld the language, culinary practices, and musical traditions of the continent from which these slaves were stolen.

We stayed on Hilton Head, in the nearby elegant resort town—my dad, my mom, my aunt Claudell, my cousin Karen, and LT Nanny, my grandmother. No one called her Grandma. L stood for Lorraine, T for Turpin, her maiden name, and Nanny was because she resisted the connotations that came with the word "grandmother." Lorraine Turpin was not old; she was not frumpy; she didn't cook or bake or knit. LT Nanny was elegant and fashionable. She was great at throwing a party. And for her, a four-star resort on swanky Hilton Head was the perfect home base for our family to explore the geography of her late husband's lineage.

We spent a lot of our time on the trip having elegant dinners and sitting by the pool, but we also rented a car to accomplish our main mission of seeing my dad's property and visiting the land from which his father hailed. I distinctly remember the stark contrast between the lush, manicured lawns of the resort on Hilton Head and the dense, wild woodlands outside its gates.

We found the land; it was an overgrown field, and as a kid from the Bronx, it was hard for me to imagine what anyone would do with it. The weather that day managed to be both humid and dusty; the air was thick with moisture, but the earth was barren and sere. I don't know what I expected, but I remember feeling underwhelmed. There was a vast silence, punctuated by the buzzing of biting insects and a dense smell of untamed wilderness. As my dad stood proudly surveying his land, I could almost see the wheels of his imagination calculating the architecture of the dreams that could be built here. I wondered how long we'd have to stand there.

Eventually, having exhausted our reasons to stay, we headed to the relief of the air-conditioned car. Finding our way back to Hilton Head proved oddly difficult, and as we pulled over to ask two men for directions, I remember struggling to understand their instructions. I'd had no problem understanding the southern drawl of the hotel staff, but for me, this roadside patois evoked a language further removed. My dad leaned in and seemed capable of deciphering their words. Once clear about where to drive next, he started to close the window, but as he did, we heard one of the men turn to the other and say, "Hilton Head?"

The other man said—and this part I understood—"Yeah—they Black folks, but they look rich."

In that moment the distance between where my grandfather was from and the life my dad was living started to become clear. And in some ways, LT Nanny stood at the gates of that divide. No one was more excited to return to the comforts of Hilton Head. And while my dad was proud to be a landowner and to stand on property passed down to him from his father, he seemed even more proud to be identified as "rich." From where I sat in that car, the appearance of wealth seemed to hold more value than the worth of the land itself. I learned that appearances matter, and that to be thought of as wealthy or powerful or successful was a goal worth pursuing, whether it was true or not.

~~~

During her brief first marriage, my mother had been devastated by the birth of a stillborn child. Her marriage had not been a happy one—her former husband had suffered from undiagnosed mental illness featuring grandiose visions and compulsive lying. The end of their marriage came after he fired a gun toward my mother's head and claimed that he had purposefully missed. (Years later, when I asked where this had happened, she said, "In your bedroom," which had been her office before I was born.)

The stillbirth had led to many unanswered questions about my mother's overall reproductive health, which had only made the loss harder to bear. But still, she was incredibly stoic. Stoicism has always been one of her talents. I often joke that she spent her entire life learning how to not have feelings, only to be gifted with a highly emotional child. But my mother wasn't cold. She was poised. Graceful. Controlled. The kind of woman you trust with a secret you want to take to the grave.

My parents got married in a small ceremony in St. Ann's Church in the South Bronx. My mother wore a pale peach-colored dress that had been crocheted by her mother; my dad wore a Merlot-colored velvet tuxedo.

After five years of trying to conceive, my mother's belly finally swelled, and my dad's pride bloomed. Their prayers had been answered. The miracle took hold.

From the start I knew that I was wanted, and I knew that I was loved. Even as a small child I was told that it had taken my parents a long time to have me. And my mother's devotion to me was undeniable, her dedication palpable, her sacrifices endless. When it came to the development of my mind, she gave me the world.

I used to sit in the back of lecture halls and watch my mother teach hundreds of students—I don't remember a time I didn't go to my mother's job. Going to her office was part of our routine, how we lived our lives with me as the only child of a working mother. Her offices and classrooms were an extension of our Bronx apartment, each just another room where I made myself at home and occupied myself with books or coloring or puzzles. She would stand in front of packed rooms, and if she started to speak and wasn't met with attentive ears, she'd put her pen down, lean into the mic, and say, "I'll wait." Sometimes, in those classes—and because she was a professor of early education—she would ask, "What would a seven-year-old think?" and I'd raise my hand from the back of the auditorium because, after all, I was the only seven-year-old in the room. If no other hands shot up, she'd call on me, much to the delight of her students.

At home, my mother was driven by immersive education, so much so that if my cousin Rahim said he was interested in sharks, we were all suddenly reading Peter Benchley's novel *Jaws* and heading to Montauk for a long weekend. When his brother, my cousin Jared, said he loved birds of prey, off we went at dawn to the Museum of Natural History to hear a lecture about red-tailed hawks in Central Park. I loved dollhouses, so we regularly went to the Museum of the City of New York to look at the miniatures, and we endeavored to build our own. My mother's years as an educator, coupled with her own deep love of learning, provided a framework that made me both curious and determined to excel. It's no wonder that those mother-daughter evenings spent standing in the long half-price ticket line in Times Square, ready to see whatever show held the best seats at the lowest prices, evolved into opportunities to pursue a life in the arts all my own. But if the learning had been born of my mother's influence, the dreaming and believing came from a different source.

My mother's disciplined intellectual curiosity lives in opposition to my dad's electric creativity. Earl Washington loves to laugh and create and dream and tell stories. He's a modern-day griot who lives in the realm of magical thinking—his, and now my, deep faith in the possibility of dreams coming true, living against all logic, despite the odds and regardless of the facts, is absolute. It defines him. And it makes him irresistible to most. (You need look no further than my Instagram feed to witness how he commands a space with charm.)

When I was a toddler, my dad took me to see my first-ever film, *Fantasia,* in a movie theater at the bottom of the Citicorp Center building in midtown Manhattan. The magical and aspirational Disney ethos of wishing upon a star and dreams coming true runs fiercely through my dad's veins and has been passed on from his heart to mine.

It's true I probably chose the job I did because of who my dad is. He taught me that anything was possible—in fact, I reached for the impossible because of how he sees the world. But how I do what I do—the work ethic and the technique and the professionalism and the drive—that's from my mother.

So, my mother's drive to educate me, mixed with my dad's endless imagination, encoded within me the artist that I would become. Today, well-researched magical realism is my job. And I feel blessed to love what I do. But even before it was my occupational calling, the ability to live in my imagination was necessary for survival, because in the reality of my day-to-day interactions with my parents, there was an inexplicable cognitive dissonance that made it impossible to fully connect.

I did not lack for food, clothing, shelter, or culture—or any number of nice things—but I longed for an authentic connection with my parents. Something was missing, something felt wrong. And as many children do, I thought that something was me. *What's wrong with me?* I asked myself, *Why* can't *I connect?* Because despite all of it—the magic of *Fantasia* and the Broadway shows and the hawks and the sharks—from an early age I knew that something stood between my parents and me, a moat filled with their whispered conversations and my unanswered questions.

At times, I felt unhappy and alone. I hungered for siblings; I noticed in other families that having a sibling relationship made people feel less lonely and more able to make sense of the homes they shared and the parents who raised them. One afternoon, when I was about ten years old, I asked my mother why my parents chose not to have more children.

"You were a long–wished for child," she said. "You were not easy to conceive."

And then, as if to silence me and end the conversation, she shared, without emotion and very matter-of-factly, that she had given birth to another child, a half sibling (though she left that detail out), but that child had been stillborn. I had no follow-up questions. I could tell that this was not an easy topic to talk about, and I felt like the proper response from me was to just be grateful that I existed.

Like so much of the information that was exchanged in my household, this truth seemed to be delivered reluctantly and was wrapped in an implicit warning — almost an entreaty — to not ask any further questions.

When I was eight years old, I asked my mother why my LT Nanny didn't like me. My mother avoided eye contact, deflected the question, and asked me, "What makes you think that?" I was beginning to recognize avoidance and denial; once again, I knew that I'd asked the wrong thing.

I understand now that perhaps my grandmother mistrusted my mother. My dad had not married a woman who resembled his mother; maybe that made LT Nanny feel rejected by him. While my grandfather joked lovingly about trying to identify the mysteries of my mother's ethnicity ("Come on, Val, where are you *really* from?"), I think LT Nanny felt greater discomfort with this woman who was so different from her in so many ways.

I have always looked more like my mom than my dad; I was bookish like her, more serious, more sensitive. Whenever I had an independent thought or an opinion, LT would call me "Sarah," for the famous turn-of-the-century Broadway actor Sarah Bernhardt, as if having a thought of my own made me excessively dramatic.

I think LT saw me as entirely my mother's child, so maybe what I sensed was my grandmother's discomfort with me, as if something about the story of our family was not quite right.

The story I knew was the one they'd told me — that I was an only child born to Earl and Valerie Washington — but I, too, had a faint but determined sense that there was more to the story, and children are natural storytellers. So I was able to create a narrative to fill in the blanks so that I could have something that resembled a cohesive inner life. I found ways to soothe my loneliness, disappearing into books and watching movies and playing make-believe. Eventually, I found my way to the stage and to film sets—places where I could be with other human beings and we could laugh together and cry together and make eye contact and breathe and say difficult things and experience joy. And live in truth. I went to the imaginary, looking for some truth.

And I found it there.

~~~

Professionally, my dad had a tough time. He worked in financial services, owned a general store, and eventually became a real estate agent. He has always had vivid dreams of success and grandeur mixed with the too-trusting heart of an intrepid entrepreneur. This has meant that over and over he has taken on exciting ventures in the hopes that they will lead to a life of wealth and ease, but more often than not, he's been disappointed.

In the mid-eighties, the Internal Revenue Service began looking into my dad's most recent employer. In exchange for leniency, they were cooperating with the government by providing information about clients who were possibly engaged in illegal activities, and in an attempt to break professional ties with his boss but remain employed, my dad went out on his own and opened United Realty. After having hit the racial glass ceiling of accomplishments at Dun & Bradstreet and seeing his general store go under, this venture became his newest opportunity to chase the American Dream. But even as a child I could sense that what in his eyes seemed like an opportunity for undeniable success was in reality a dingy basement retail space on a rundown corner of the Grand Concourse, a once glamorous and elegant strip in the Bronx that was by then riddled with crime and addiction.

As a kid, I wondered at my dad's pride in this space. Each morning he dressed in dark suits with silk ties and spent close to an hour carefully coiffing his conservative, low Afro with gentle taps from all angles while he drank his coffee, shined his shoes, and read the *New York Daily News*. While working at Dun & Bradstreet a decade earlier, he had learned how to look the part of a successful businessman, even if the racism and prejudice of the time prevented him from actually becoming one—as just one example, he'd diligently trained an Asian American man who was then promoted ahead of him. What he lacked in luck and opportunity, he made up for in style and flair.

When asked why he loved the United Realty office space that he and his partner shared, his answer would always begin by exalting its location as a corner with high pedestrian traffic, making it an attractive draw to passersby. But observation could tell you that the heavy feet that shuffled past those basement windows did not belong to potential buyers swimming in disposable income. Most of the foot traffic belonged to the unhoused or neighborhood folks whose last concern was the accumulation of real estate. The space itself was dark. The walls were, I could tell, once white, but now gray with the dinge of time. The carpet was dirty and dotted with rat droppings. When I found myself forced to spend time in that space, only the glow of my dad's pride made it bearable. "United Realty" he would sing self-importantly, lifting the receiver to his ear whenever the telephone rang. United Realty was going to be his chance to soar. The space belonged to him. This company was his.

But in later years, in smaller spaces, with tighter overheads and limited returns, the refrain shortened to a clipped and urgent "United." This was a shorthand necessitated by a man desperately chasing a dream that he feared might never come true.

When I started talking about my family in therapy for the first time, in college, my concerns and complaints were exclusively about my dad. I would rant for entire sessions about the lack of understanding I had for him—how different we were, how often disconnected. Like many eighteen-year-olds, I thought I knew everything and my dad knew nothing. My therapist suggested that at some point I might be ready to discuss my mother, too. I looked at her as though she were insane. Later I would come to understand that there were, of course, nuances to unpack and understand about my mother, but the tension and disconnect I felt with my dad were more obvious to me at first. I didn't understand him, and he didn't understand, or fully approve of, me. Even as a young child, I felt that I was never who my dad needed me to be. I knew he really wanted a son and that they weren't having any more children. I wondered if I could soften the blow somehow by being a daughter who was prettier, or smarter, or braver, or more successful, but even that didn't work. In the instances he actually made it to a choral performance, for example, he would always ask me if we had been slightly off-key. Eventually, I stopped trying to live up to what seemed like my dad's impossible standards. I decided that I could not mitigate his dissatisfaction with life by being perfect. Instead, I rejected him and his opinions. I tried to be perfect for everyone else.

～～

When I was sixteen, I was at dinner with my mother and her sister Daphne. We were in the Whitestone section of the Bronx, a historically Italian neighborhood. Sinatra and his cronies serenaded us through the speakers as other families—locals, regulars—laughed and ate their marinara, marsala, piccata, and pesto.

My aunt "Daph" is my "other mother"—she's the only other woman (besides my mother-in-law) who receives presents and cards from me on Mother's Day. She is the youngest of my mother's four sisters and two brothers, and my mother's closest ally. They say it takes a village to raise a child; Aunt Daph was the most esteemed dignitary in the village that raised me, and her sons, Rahim and Jared, were my brothers.

At some point that evening, the conversation turned to my dad and the frustrations he was causing in our home. It was the same conversation, again and again. He didn't contribute. He didn't provide. He was wasting money that we couldn't afford to spare. I decided that night that I had endured enough of my mother's complaints.

"Mom," I said. "Come on! If you're this unhappy, why don't you leave him? Why not just get a divorce?"

My mother looked across the table at her sister. She slowly forced her gaze back to me and took a long, sad inhale. She seemed to be trying to muster the strength to clear a pathway for reality.

"Because I can't," she said. "If I kick him out, he'll have nothing."

Her eyes were filled with regret and remorse; she seemed trapped in a prison of her own compassion and guilt. And saddened to admit it all. As miserable as she may have been at different points in their marriage, my mother was unable to inflict the kind of pain on my dad that she said he had placed on her and on our home. She may not have had much in the way of resources, but still she felt that he had less.

CHAPTER TWO

FISH

I grew up in the Bronx, on a street named after a creek that used to run through its marshy woodlands and feed into the nearby East River. Pugsley Creek, originally Maeneppis Kill, was a small waterway used by the Siwanoys, a tribe of Indigenous Americans, to reach their village near the tip of Castle Hill Neck. But in the 1800s, the Pugsley family acquired large swaths of land in the area and used the creek to ship supplies to and from their sprawling farm. Eventually, as the southeast sections of the Bronx were developed, much of the land was filled in and the now-named Pugsley Creek was shortened.

By the time my mother found our two-bedroom on Pugsley Avenue, there was no evidence of the tiny waterway within our direct view. But water was still all around us. Looking out from our living room windows, in the distance beyond the Castle Hill Projects and at the very end of the Cross Bronx Expressway, we had a view of the Whitestone Bridge suspended across the East River. And straight down below us was the crown jewel of my block, the summer haven of our neighborhood, the Jamie Towers pool.

My parents and I lived on the twelfth, and highest, floor of Building Four in Jamie Towers. The towers are one of the famed Mitchell-Lama buildings in New York City. The Mitchell-Lama Program, named after former New York state senator MacNeil Mitchell and former assemblyman Alfred Lama and made into law in 1955, was established to create "affordable rental and cooperative housing to moderate- and middle-income families," according to New York City Housing Preservation & Development. Although our buildings were subsidized by government dollars, at "Jamie"—as we affectionately called our home—we held on to a belief that we were not living in government housing, aka "the projects." That term would be reserved for the collections of buildings just across from Building One on Olmstead Avenue. Enormous consideration and maintenance were poured into the facilities in an attempt to make sure that they looked and felt different from the Castle Hill or nearby Bronx River projects.

Our neighborhood, like many neighborhoods in the Bronx, was filled with hardworking families reaching toward the American Dream. The architecture wasn't as complex or sophisticated as, say, Co-op City, a few miles to the north, and it didn't have the historic art deco design or history of Parkchester, but like those developments, Jamie did have a strong sense of community.

When it was built, Jamie was designed for people who felt they were at the gateway of the middle class. It featured tall glass entryways, state-of-the-art closed-circuit cameras, and sprawling green lawns with gardens and play structures. There were four buildings, each named after a literary giant. My building, Building Four, was named not for Phillis Wheatley or Langston Hughes, but for the arch colonialist Rudyard Kipling. Mostly these buildings were identical, with tiny differentiating features in their common spaces. The room at the bottom of Building Three, for example, was our community room, used to fulfill many of the needs of the block—from voting booths on Election Day to weddings, Halloween parties, or meetings of the Jamie Towers Board Association.

The most important committee at Jamie Towers was the one in charge of the Jamie Towers pool—our beloved outdoor pool, cradled in concrete, resting in the middle of Jamie's four towering apartment buildings.

～～

My parents' love of water seemed to guide their relationship and be passed onto me, somehow; perhaps genetically transferred into my bones.

My favorite picture of us as a family is one of my parents and me as a toddler sitting together on the warm concrete at the Jamie Towers pool. We are all smiling at the camera, caught in that special kind of joy and laughter that emanates from a soul after it's had time to sink and float and dive and play in water. In the photo, we are huddled together on the side of the pool farthest from the lifeguard station and closest to our building. We are just outside the gated "kiddie pool" area.

The geography of the photo is striking to me. We some-times sat in that section of the pool if a member of our extended family was having a birthday party or celebrating a graduation or an anniversary or some other rite of passage, because that side of the pool had a corrugated tin canopied enclosure made for shade. Maybe it was taken at a party for my cousin Rahim's birthday? His birthday, which falls on July 4, was always celebrated with extra fervor because while no slaves were free on Independence Day in 1776, Rahim's birthday gave us an excuse to gather, celebrate, barbecue, and watch fireworks all the same. There's no evidence of a party in the picture, but there is really no other reason why we would have been so close to the kiddie pool—I have no memories of splashing or wading in there. I never swam in it. From as young as eighteen months old, I headed straight for the main pool, jumped into the deep end, and stayed there throughout most of my childhood.

I remember being in the pool, surrounded by crystal blue threads of light shimmering all around me; I remember the sounds of other kids laughing, playing, splashing. I remember a whistle blowing in the distance because someone was running, much to the annoyance of a lifeguard. I have no memories of not being able to swim, no recollection of learning how to move underwater. Being in water, moving through water, has always felt more natural to me than walking on land. When I am in the water, I am at peace, and when I am submerged, between breaths, I feel most at home with myself, in my body. As a child, even when I hated my body, I loved being in the water. I remember going to my mother one day in my bathing suit and pointing out the protruding shape of my belly as a flaw I wanted to fix. She said, "Just hold in your tummy. That's what everyone does."

So, on land, in my bathing suit, I learned to restrict my body, to hold my breath, and to pretend. But in the water, I could be free.

I have always loved the ways in which water manipulates sound. The way noise races across the surface, amplifying sound for miles, and then the muffled distance created by being underwater. This so often feels like an escape to me because the world gets quieter, my heartbeat grows louder, and my thoughts and feelings become precise, clear. When I'm stressed, swimming allows me a safe route out of myself, helping me to escape my thoughts and then return to a calmer, more centered version of me.

One of my earliest memories is of my mother regularly imploring me to use my arms to swim. At the time, like a lot of kids who learn to swim by instinct and not via formal training, I moved quickly like a mermaid, or a tadpole, powered by rhythmic shimmies and swirls. Each bright summer morning, from a time before I can remember, I would move my tiny body through the water in the way that felt most comfortable and efficient, but still my mother would ask, "Why don't you use your arms?"

Even at three, I could sense in her question a suggestion that what I was doing was wrong and an invitation to discover how to be better. But I was a little girl whom the lifeguards called

"Fish"—I wanted to just go about life moving and grooving through the water in the ways that felt easiest and most natural for me.

Again and again she would pose that question: "Why don't you use your arms?" Posing it in the negative forced me to think it through for myself, to be curious and questioning of my ways. Finally, one afternoon, the siren song of the unknown got the best of me, and I surrendered to the experiment. *Use my arms how?* I thought. While treading water—I was too tiny to stand and touch my toes at even the shallowest end of the pool— I thought about the movements that I had seen grown-ups make when they swam. The movement that seemed easiest for me to emulate was the reach swimmers make with their arms stretched out ahead of them, pushing the water behind them like snow angels, looking down into the water and flying upstream. I swooshed the water down the sides of my body, letting my heart lead me forward, and learned that with my arms engaged, I had twice as many muscles and ligaments to move me through space.

My mother's guidance made me better. Faster. And stronger. I felt even more powerful and free in the water than I had before. On land, my instructions had been to remain small. But in water I was discovering a different part of myself. And I was learning to bring all of me into this particular effort. My mother's urgings had opened a world of possibility, and like the brilliant educator that she was, she let me find it on my own and in my own time so that I was ready to learn it.

Leaning into my curiosity is perhaps the single most important tool my mother has given me. Swimming in the deep end is most definitely my superpower.

~~~

When the school year ended, we counted the days until the Jamie Towers pool would be opened for the summer. And when it was, my cousins and I would often be the first to arrive in the morning, before the lifeguards even came to unlock the gate. We would wait impatiently on the pavement, our noses pressed against the fencing. At the top of that gate were spirals of barbed wire. They'd been put in place around the pool only after the pool committee—which my mother was on, of course—voted to install them to prevent the teenagers from the Castle Hill projects from breaking into the pool and swimming at night. I remember standing in my parents' bedroom, gazing out of the small window on my mother's side of the bed. There, below, I had seen them: Boys, older than me, taller and more adventurous for sure, climbing the gates and jumping into the pool with no lifeguard on duty to stop them.

Entry into the Jamie Towers pool was not a given—you needed a membership ID card. These were printed on thin pastel pieces of cardboard that indicated you had paid your fees and were in good standing. There were different colors for different types of membership and a limited number of passes made for guests. We would stand at the gate and wait until Manny or Joseph or one of the other lifeguards arrived, and then we would racewalk (because one of the rules of the pool was "No running!") to find our favorite spot on the concrete and spread out our towels before digging into our pockets to pull out our IDs. The lifeguards on duty would take our IDs and place them in a silver box until the end of the day. But some summers they just kept our IDs on file and barely asked for them. We were native fixtures at the pool, like the ladders and filters and the signs that stipulated the rules.

Food was "not permitted" inside the gates, but no one ever challenged a kid who quickly inhaled a sandwich while hiding under a towel draped over her head like a ghost under a sheet on Halloween. I still remember the way sunlight would seep through the tiny threads of cotton and cast a warm glow within my makeshift lunch tent. My sandwiches were usually toast with butter, grape jelly, and American cheese. My allergy to tree nuts led us to believe that I was also allergic to peanuts, so no peanut butter. But the tangy, sweet combination of cheese and jelly never felt like a consolation prize. I liked the way the sugar of the Smucker's and the salty, smooth flavors of the cheese and butter melded together in my mouth. And I loved being different and special, loved having a sandwich that was unique to me. We ate with our eyes half closed against the high sun, our bodies aching and soaked in chlorine.

One summer, we were signed up for a day camp within walking distance of Jamie Towers, at the Kips Bay Boys & Girls Club. A couple of days a week, the day camp would walk all its campers across the two long city blocks and over to Jamie to enjoy the swimming pool for an hour before it was opened to the public. Those days were magical. Every hour of swimming was precious, every minute golden. To have advanced private entry felt like we were cheating the gods and being granted a favor we didn't deserve. Even when we had to leave the pool and pack up to head to camp, our private access had made it all worthwhile.

On longer days at the pool, however, we dreaded the twice daily "adult swims." As an adult now, I appreciate the ritual of creating a moment in the day where grown-ups can swim laps in the pool without being chased and splashed and interrupted by the games of children. But at the time, this forced break in our swimming elicited only disdain. Twice a day, the lifeguards blew their whistles and shouted for us to "Get outta the water!" And then, for forty-five minutes, we were forced back onto land and into the heaviness of our limbs, our hunger, and whatever worries the buoyancy of the water had allowed us to escape. Wanting to spend the time strategically, we would often use the minutes of "adult swim" to head upstairs for a snack, or if we were lucky enough to have money in our pockets, we would race up the street to grab a slice of pizza. And on the very best of days, a miracle of all miracles would occur, and the singsong jingle of the ice cream truck would emerge beneath the cruel whistle of the lifeguards. That happy song, the sound of urban summer sweetness, would make the minutes of adult swim fly by. And at the end of the forty-five minutes, our hands sticky and lips stained from the tint of Bomb Pop ice pops, we'd head back into our magical place with the adults banished, and the pool all ours again.

A coveted privilege at the pool was to be the one child chosen to reinstate the floating rope that got pulled in for adult swim and would be used afterward as the divider between deep and shallow waters. If you were chosen, you got to dive in and put the rope back in place just before the whistle signaled the end of adult swim—so in that moment, you were granted the solitary privilege of being a child in grown-up waters, and, crucially, someone who had more time in the water than anyone else that day.

~~~

Before I was born, my mother had lived with her first husband, Mike Godfrey, in the same apartment that I grew up in. There, she developed lesson plans while he painted; they read and listened to music; and they fought. Once my mother became pregnant, she and Mike transformed their second bedroom into a nursery, filled with gifts from friends and family who were excited about their coming bundle of joy.

My mother now says that she always knew, somewhere deep in the recesses of her heart, that there might be a problem with the pregnancy. Her stomach stopped broadening, and the flutters of movement began to quiet. Having never been pregnant before, she convinced herself that maybe she had been blessed with an extremely calm child. But when it was time to deliver, the baby was born with great difficulty and no heartbeat. After the heartbreaking birth of their stillborn child in 1968, Mike tortured my mother by painting portrait after portrait of a pregnant woman with an empty womb, filled only by a black pool of longing, an empty embryonic abyss. Such cruelty could not be borne, and they divorced. But my mother kept the apartment at Jamie Towers and turned the nursery back into an office — this time for herself, a room of her own.

Nine years later, that same room would be turned once again into a nursery, but this time for me.

~⌒~

Because apartment 12D was on the top floor, facing the borough of Queens on the other side of the river, we lived beneath one of the direct flight paths to LaGuardia Airport. Sometimes, while standing in the apartment or out on the steel-framed terrace, aircraft would slice through the sky and appear to be flying right into our living room. As I stood steady, gazing skyward, I'd watch pilots skim the rooftops of our neighborhood again and again and fantasize about being on those planes. I wanted to go on an adventure; I longed to travel. I hungered for the ability to be anywhere other than in that apartment alone, an only child and a latchkey kid. And the truth was, even when there were people around — for example, if my cousins were with me after school, or when my parents came home from work in the evenings — no matter who else was there, I still felt deeply alone. It was a sinking feeling, and I wanted to soar. So, I eventually found a way to escape, even if only in my mind.

These were the days of compact disc players, and in my living room I would pick a song and grab a hairbrush and sing entire concerts to my imaginary crowd of thousands.

Sometimes, as if in a movie montage, my performance would morph into a music video in which I would build characters to support the narrative of the song. Other songs called for me to be center stage, alone in a spotlight. I would pretend to be Natalie Cole singing *Unforgettable*: the entire album, beginning to end, while dancing across my living room, pausing only to interact with an imaginary band and the ghost of my father.

My parents also had a collection of Motown ballads called *Endless Love*. When I wasn't performing the title track with an imaginary male suitor, my next favorite song from the album was "I've Never Been to Me" by Charlene, a song whose lyrics—with references to unborn children and discontented mothers—evoked some deep emotional truth for me, even without my full understanding of their adult themes (feel free to Google "subtle whoring").

But in the real world, my travels were local. For half of my elementary education, I went to a neighborhood school one block away from Jamie Towers. P.S. 182 sat on the other side of Stevenson High School's sprawling running track and football field, which were just across the street from our front door. P.S. 182 was built the year I was born. The walls were covered in shiny bright tiles; the play structures pristine and unscarred. There was a large recess yard, a smaller play area, a lunchroom filled with light, a talented and gifted program, and upstairs, the superintendent's office for all of District 8.

One day when I was in kindergarten, I told my mother that I wanted to walk to school by myself and she let me, even though it was 1983 and in the light of morning, on blocks like ours, there was no way to ignore the graphic remnants of crack paraphernalia all around. Tiny vials with colorful caps were everywhere you looked; occasionally you could spy fragments of a stained-glass pipe. Traveling that long sidewalk by myself, hopscotching over jagged fissures in the concrete, I felt like a grown-up — strong, capable, self-reliant, and in control. Unbeknownst to me, however, my mother had followed me, at a distance, all the way there. The secrets began early in my family; they were secrets designed to protect me, and to do what my parents thought was best for me. But they were secrets all the same. My mother was very good at this, excellent at the gamification of important tasks. Whenever she slammed the trunk of a car closed, she'd say, "Cover your ears — there's going to be a loud noise!"

It took me years to realize that she wasn't really protecting our ears — she was cleverly making sure no little fingers got caught.

My mother was, to say the least, an involved parent. Given her deep understanding of the education system, she also became a parent activist. At times the superintendent would stop me in the halls to ask if she'd dropped me at school that day. Some days, like that day in kindergarten, I'd tell him that I walked alone, and the superintendent always seemed to brighten when I said that. I thought he was proud of me for being so responsible — little did I know he was actually relieved because he was terrified of my mother, who was always advocating for change and demanding higher standards for our school.

Eventually, an initiative developed to move the talented and gifted (TAG) program from P.S. 182 about four miles north, to P.S. 71 in the mostly white Pelham Bay section of the Bronx. In those days, the student body at P.S. 71 was almost entirely Italian American—Columbus Day was their biggest holiday of the year. Underlying the move of the program was the sentiment from white parents that they did not want to bus their children into a predominantly Black and Latine section of the Bronx. My mother and my friend Tomiko's mom were both educators and adamantly against the move, so the school board simply waited until both were absent from a meeting before taking the vote. Without their voices in the room to represent the families of color in the TAG program, who outnumbered the white families, the proposal passed. The Black and Latine students, myself included, would now carry the burden of inconvenience, and face a longer commute into a different world.

So, for my final years of elementary school I was being bused to the other side of town. Even though we had very similar lives and upbringings—many of our grandparents had come through Ellis Island in the twenties and thirties, and many of our parents were treading water in the space between working- and middle-class—this would be the first time that I would start to feel truly othered. At P.S. 71, almost all the kids of color were the students in the special education programs and those of us in the TAG classes—pretty much everyone else was Italian American. To a child of color, the message was clear: You had to be exceptional. You could either be excellent or require special needs. Otherwise, you'd get lost.

Even at this young age I was already struggling with the feeling of not being good enough. The move to P.S. 71 exacerbated these feelings. When Valentine's Day approached, none of the boys even remotely considered asking me to be their valentine or to receive their thin cardboard gestures. My new best friend, Jennifer, on the other hand, was inundated with them, or so it seemed to me. Signs of othering were everywhere. At the age of nine I couldn't quite put my finger on what exactly it all meant, but I knew what it felt like. It reeked of limitations and restrictions, of being undesirable, of being kept on the outside and being forced to look in at what you could not have.

In my final year at P.S. 71, I auditioned for the sixth-grade musical, *Bye Bye Birdie.* Secretly, I wanted to land the role of Kim MacAfee, the lead character, but when my teacher asked why I didn't audition for it, I told her that I knew I wouldn't get it because I wasn't white. The part I snagged was that of Rose Alvarez. This was no consolation prize. This was one of the important characters of the show—a role that had been originated by Chita Rivera, for which she'd been nominated for a Tony Award. But what I also understood was that this was an "ethnic" role, and a "supporting" one. I was being told that my job was not to be the main character in the story, but to assist her.

~~

When people ask me if I am the first actor in my family, I often joke that I am just the first to get paid for it. There are no other professional performing artists in our family tree that I know

of, but we—my mom, my dad, and me—are a family of performers. Each of us has spent a lifetime playing a role vital to
our shared narrative. My role in our performance came naturally because I was born into its twists and turns and draped
in its masks and costumes. We three were the picture-perfect
presentation of ourselves as we wanted to be perceived not only
by the outside world, but by each other. We were a fairy-tale
portrait of success. And this was the only show I knew—
we performed it all day long, and for years. This script was how
we tried to avoid pain, messiness, and discomfort.

The thing about an illusion is that, unless you are the
magician, you don't always see the trick when you are inside
of it. My dad and mom were the magician and his assistant,
and I was the audience member who had been invited onto the
stage to be cut in half. I had no window into the secrets of how
the trick had been performed, but I smiled and waved and
received the applause in any case, knowing that without me,
their act was incomplete. So, we dressed our part and performed our fairy tale, but like a princess hidden away in Jamie
Towers, I knew that there was more to the story that I had yet
to discover, more to my life that had yet to unfold.

We were a family that colored inside the lines. We were
innovators and entrepreneurs, but we were not rule breakers.
We were the family that voted for barbed wire around our precious pool and called security when those boys dove into the
deep end in the middle of the night. We desperately wanted to
control the chaos that threatened our sense of safety. We would
do almost anything to protect the illusion of our perfection.

Now, as an adult, one of my favorite things to do with my family in the summertime is take a night swim. In the warm evening air that visits Los Angeles in our hottest months, we revel in the freedom of soaring and tumbling under the stars. Swimming at bedtime is, to me, the ultimate fantasy of rule breaking and freedom, like sleeping in a museum, or eating your dessert before your dinner (something that, incidentally, my husband does at restaurants all the time!). There, in the deep end, I can behold the dancing shadows of my kids as they frolic in the water, their laughter bouncing across the ripples, and I pray that they feel safer than I did. Not safer in the water—in the water I had always felt held and protected by the element itself. My prayer is that their spirits remain as powerful and buoyant on land as they are in the water. And in the light of day as well as at night.

CHAPTER THREE

MAGICAL THINKING

When I was a child, things were different for me at night. At night, I tossed and turned, knowing that something was not quite as it seemed and that things were happening that were dangerously wrong. With the day's performance over, the curtains drawn, the theater empty, I stayed up to see what ghosts haunted the stage. And there, in those late-night hours, I sometimes met my mom and dad without their masks, angry beasts with no audience to pretend for anymore.

There was yelling and crying, but only when they thought I was asleep. The next morning, they'd smile and pretend all was fine.... So, I, too, learned to smile, to cover for them, to pretend—to resist the call to see what was really going on. I learned to be someone else early on, my people-pleasing skills honed on those mornings when nothing was deemed amiss. I learned to keep my parents happy so that I would be safe.

But something was still off. And I blamed myself.

~~~

From what I remember, most of the fights were about money, and about the fact that neither of my parents felt like they were in the marriage they wanted to be in, or more precisely, that neither was married to the person they wanted to be married to. They argued about my dad's spending versus my mother's thriftiness; my dad's failures to earn versus my mother's failure of ambition; my dad's regular absences versus my mother's obsession with me.

They both harbored deep disappointment over what their lives had become—my mother was disappointed in my dad, and my dad was disappointed in the marriage. I developed a sense that I was the only thing keeping them together, or that I had to try to be. I was supposed to deliver them to happiness, to avoid triggering in them any emotion even close to disappointment. So, when they fought, I took it as my failure, and felt like it was my job to fix it.

Like a lot of families, the magic trick was in the pretending. We pretended to ourselves, to each other, and to the outside world that our family was not suffering the pain of life's disappointments. We were fine—but I learned a long time ago that FINE can be an acronym for fucked-up, insecure, neurotic, and emotional.

Despite her previous marriage (a marriage I only discovered when I was twelve years old and stumbled upon pictures of my mother wearing a wedding dress and standing next to a man who was not my dad), despite both of their professional struggles that I didn't yet understand, and despite the hidden legal battles that consumed them both—despite all of this, the show went on. And again, I learned that appearances mattered, and what mattered most was the appearance of being OK.

There were other characters in our drama, too. Beyond money and my parents' compatibility, my dad's drinking played a powerful role in our family dynamics, though it was not a problem as far as he was concerned. From his perspective, he drank for fun, and with great flair. And he was working—"networking"—till late hours, getting increasingly entertaining with each drink. I'd seen this behavior on holidays and at family functions and I grew to dread this version of my dad—boundaryless, gregarious, and self-important. In a world where he struggled to find the kind of material success and power that he craved, drinking allowed the big-boss-man persona within him to be the center of every circle and the life of every party. Back at home, my mother, weary of the familiar ways that alcohol distorted and destroyed the family she had been born into, didn't meet his performances with the same appreciative audience that he found in happy-hour bars. There was no tipsy crowd celebrating and applauding him in apartment 12D. So, on many nights, he stayed out late, found comfort in the warmth of laughter, and came home sloppy.

Later, when I was in high school and a few of my dad's bars were on my way to rehearsal, I feared that I would bump into him in his more inebriated state. Wanting to shortcut that horror, I would conjure the scenario in my head, auditioning the embarrassment and rehearsing the dread so as not to be surprised when overcome with it. The fear only heightened when, as I got older, my friends and I found our own way into bars with the help of fake IDs or flirtatious bouncers. Once inside, my imagination would again go to work. In the scene that unfolded in my mind, I would be engaged in illegal underage drinking, and he would be holding court across the room. Usually, in my imagination, my dad had his arm draped suggestively around a woman, someone who was not my mother, and as our eyes met from across the bar, we would see each other — both of us transgressing and witnessing each other's transgressions.

What began in my mind as a test run for trauma eventually began to feel like a fantasy of freedom. I wondered if acknowledging each other's sins might create a place of shared peace between us. Such a moment would have released us from so much pretending. Maybe then we could *really* see each other, accept each other, forgive each other, and move on. I longed for some raw, unbridled truth to be laid bare between us. The daydream was so frequent that I began to believe that it had actually happened. I think deep down I wished that it had. But instead, the pretending that we did for each other became the lies that I told myself. And like my dad, I was getting good at make-believe.

My dad adored me, and partly because of that love, he created a false reality about me. Even as I was assimilating many of my dad's coping mechanisms — like magical thinking and using substances to escape reality — I did not understand them. Or him. At times I could not fathom how we were even related. He seemed, sometimes, like a foreign figure from a strange land. I belonged to him, but I was not of him. I felt, in some ways, trapped by his love, occasionally appalled by his desperation, then always ashamed. Ashamed of not being a better daughter. Of not being more loving or kind. Of not connecting more deeply and wholeheartedly.

Most nights when my dad came home, I hid in my room pretending to be asleep. I knew, by heart, the song of his sloppy shuffle across the wood-paneled floor. And as I listened, I wondered just how he'd made it. One of the many miracles of my dad's existence was the Jamie Towers parking spot that he was assigned. In an outdoor expanse that fit hundreds of cars, somehow Earl Washington had been assigned a space that, while being the full length of the lot away from the entry gate, was also directly in front of that gate. To avoid disaster, all he had to do every night was glide straight ahead into his spot. And as if God hadn't given him enough, that spot was beneath the only signage in the entire lot—a shiny and reflective white traffic sign that dictated the lot's five-mile-per-hour speed limit. It was a beacon for my dad in his blurry state.

Once upstairs, there were three possible ways that the night might unfold. If my mother and I were both awake, a delicate dance began. In my younger years, my mother would instruct me to be patient and "nice" to my dad, to not say too much that might upset him. With the jangle of his keys in the top and bottom locks, she would turn to me, smile apologetically, and give me a coded warning. Sometimes the warning was marked by a kiss on my forehead or a nudge for me to head toward my bedroom. But as I got older, she knew that I knew what was on the other side of that door, so together we would watch for signs and gauge our movements based on my dad's level of intoxication and its attendant hubris.

If I was in the middle of doing something when my dad walked in—finishing my homework, clearing the table, or simply sitting between my mother's legs as she braided my hair or put hard plastic rollers in it—I would watch my mother's transformation as she steeled herself for his homecoming. Her spine would stiffen; her breath became shallow and fatigued. Her movements grew tenser, and a veil would descend across her eyes.

I was no stranger to my mother's protective veils. She had one for me, too. But this was different. Unlike the veil that she deployed to keep me from being able to read her innermost thoughts, the veil induced by my dad was designed to keep my mother's rage trapped deep inside her. The veil that greeted me was sheer and fluid—it obscured her from me, created a distance between us that was necessary for her to maintain her secrets, but it never entirely hid my mother from my view. The veil that existed between her and my dad, though? That was ironclad. Night after night, I watched my mother gird herself with emotional armor on the inside while remaining calm and stoic on the outside, almost as if a warmer, gentler portrait of herself was painted on the surface of her mask.

This performance, this presentation of herself, was not that of a wife, disappointed and disgruntled. She often tried, at least at first, to project some other, more peaceful version of herself into the situation to diffuse the potential for confrontation between them. So, whatever my dad saw when he walked in the door, this was not my mother's truth. It was a mask, a performance. The dialogue, and the blocking, were an exercise in avoidance. She seemed to decide that this man was not deserving of her truth, and that the easiest way to get through this moment, this evening, this marriage, and perhaps this lifetime was to keep him out and communicate from behind the mask.

Even though I was a child, and understood as a child might, I could see beyond my mother's armor. I could see so much compassion, still, in the performance, or at least as much as she could muster. My mother treated my dad with the gentle detachment of an emergency room nurse. She approached the patient carefully, unable to immediately gauge the level of danger he posed, but nonetheless determined to somehow provide adequate, if not quite loving, care.

I was fascinated by their dance. She was the resistant and resentful snake charmer, and he was her viper prepared to poison. He came home with slurred speech and sour breath, already missing his friends at the bar, the ones who never complained and who celebrated his charms. She wrangled his ego, constantly pirouetting through the land mine of its discontent, unclear that she would ever escape it. I was their audience, watching attentively with a keen eye for the cues that would lead me into the best version of my own dance. I learned to hide like my mother, duck away from his sloppy affections, and ignore remarks that didn't make sense. When he tugged at the conversational rope between them, I watched her set her side of the rope down and understood that in doing so, she had kept the peace by averting another verbal battle.

As I got older and my mother realized I was growing less comfortable in my costume, the recipes for compliance and avoidance that she used to whisper to me turned into more stern instructions or mildly desperate directives.

"Please don't provoke him," she would say, and I would roll my eyes. Or, if the phone call that he sometimes made on the way home indicated that the alcohol had impacted not just his speech but likely his attitude, she would say, sharply, "Just go to bed. Quickly."

Her disgust with him became more palpable. Her patience waned, even with me.

I was disgusted, too. I grew resentful of his outsized ego, which swelled when he'd been drinking. Unlike my mother, I had not spoken vows that guaranteed loyalty to him, but like her, I still felt the pressure to treat him with love. Moment to moment I was confused by the whiplash of contradictory emotions that his drinking inspired. Maybe it was because I, too, sensed a deep vulnerability in him, his profound need to love and be loved. Maybe I felt the urge to provide loving-kindness when it appeared that my mother could not.

At times, my parents both seemed powerless to me. My mother was powerless over him, and he, if not over alcohol itself, then perhaps over the entire culture of "happy hour." And it was true that his personal and professional worlds were unpredictable—but "happy hour" always came with consistent and inevitable rewards. These were rewards that he lived for but didn't get at home: joy, adulation, and escapism. He became not only tipsy from the alcohol but drunk from all the inebriated love, acceptance, and praise, too. The bartenders and the patrons only got the version of him that he chose to show them: friendly, generous, entertaining, brilliant, well connected, even wise.

My mother and I could never compete with the good feelings that flooded those bars. If circumstances made it impossible for me to scurry away and avoid contact with my dad, I would be forced to engage with the version of him that had been drinking, and every second tore my insides to shreds. Even though this version of my dad was often difficult to understand, it was also the version of him that most wanted to connect and experience closeness. And I knew it. I wanted to be patient with him; I wanted to be kind. But watching my mother masterfully hide her rage in those earlier years gave me surprising permission to cultivate my own.

Outside our home, my dad was a hero. Inside the walls of our tiny Bronx enclave, he was a tragedy seemingly unaware of the real drama unfolding around him. If I was asleep when my dad came home, but my mother was awake, the drama could not be denied. Without the audience of a child's eyes, there was less reason for her to don the mask that protected me from her rage. If I was asleep, there was nothing left to hold back their anger with each other, no reason to behave. If I was asleep, there was more space for these lovers who had become enemies to go to war.

Which meant that I usually did not remain asleep.

I once asked my mother if my parents had ever had a happy marriage. Indignant, she scoffed, "We were happy for many years. We had many, many good years before you came along and many good years that you are just too young to remember." What most struck me about her answer was how much history lived in the story of my parents' love. Her answer reminded me that even as a teenager, whatever years of discontent I thought I knew were predated by perhaps a decade of something else. Something that held them together even now. As a teenager, I would watch my dad's hand reach for my mother's and would see her stiffen in an effort not to recoil. But before this, it seemed there was a time when her body would lean into his, when perhaps his touch was more welcome. A time filled with love, adventure, courage, and dreams. I was the result of those times, wasn't I? I was one of those dreams come true.

But at night, when they fought, it was as if they were chasing other dreams, dreams that lay just out of reach. Looking back, once I learned the truth about how long the IRS had been investigating my dad, I realized that it was the IRS that had been a main predator of their dreams. Tensions rose, as did their legal fees and their darkest fears. And as they slammed doors and shouted obscenities at each other, I could feel the tension between them, vibrating through the wall.

As a young child, I would lie in bed and listen for signs of how serious each battle was and when it might come to an end. Sometimes the entire "fight" would consist of my mother slamming a door to signal that she was done. But sometimes the yelling carried on.

~~∾~~

I developed panic attacks at night. They manifested first as a rhythm of anxiety that encircled my brain, then evolved into a rapid pulsing, a whirling frenzy of metallic thumps, like those nauseating old spinning rides at a county fair.

This was not just a feeling. It was a sound, an internal beat, or series of beats, though they didn't equate to music. It was the sound of terror, wholly unnatural and unconnected to the rhythms of my heart. I was dizzied with fear, no ground beneath me; it was crazy-making, endless. And sad. There was something so sad about the rhythm. And I couldn't make it stop. I couldn't sleep. It was as though the alarms within me had been triggered and there was no turning them off.

I was seven years old.

It wasn't every single night, but even on peaceful nights, I trembled at the possibility of it. Lying in bed, I would race to fall asleep before the sounds would leak from my bones. I would force myself to try to have "good" thoughts. I hated that the rhythm came from within me. I hated that my own brain was not to be trusted. If I lost the race to sleep and got caught by the rhythm, I had no tools to escape it, no way of controlling my own brain as it conspired against me.

I tried everything to avoid it. If I could sense it coming on, from deep within my cells, I would try to sing a song, or recite a poem, or do anything I could think of to simply turn my brain off. But it would take hold in my fascia, then work outward through my muscles and tendons. Sometimes, I would rock my body back and forth, vibrating, rattling, trying to drown out the pulsing noise and regain control of my body. Sometimes I would put my head under a pillow, trying to ignore the fact that the torture was coming from within me.

But only exhaustion would override the rhythm, lulling me to the dream state beyond my fears.

I would fight the haunting rhythm as it rose in me, often having to compete with my parents' fights in the next room. If my inner rhythm won, I was tortured by the tempo of my own obsessive brain; if my parents' arguing won, I was trapped by fear. One night around that time, I hurled the pillow to the ground in frustration. I knew that my job was to hide, to stay in my room and pretend that this was not happening—I understood that they were only fighting because they believed that I was asleep. If I let on that I was awake, well then, I'd be disrupting the roles as they had been written.

But I needed something from them, too—I needed them to stop fighting because I wanted to feel safe.

Part of me wanted them to know that I knew, that I heard them, that I was not being fooled by the smiles the next morning, by the whispers and the denials of their pain. I wanted to be in truth, even then. That night, the pillow thrown to the floor, I'd had enough—I went out into the living room and yelled, "Stop! Please stop!"

They stood still, perhaps in shock. My dad had been drinking; he was at the far end of our narrow kitchen. My mother stood across from him in the corner of our cramped living room, close to the door that led to our small terrace.

Even then I could sense my mother's frustrated desperation. She looked at me for what seemed like forever, and then she started to cry. In my life, I can count on one hand the number of times that I have seen my mother cry; this was the second. As she wiped her tears, she seemed to me to be sinking, drowning in an abyss of sadness. The mask she wore for my dad, and for me when my dad was around, had fallen away, washed off hours ago in the rage of their argument. But he was not done — he moved to the center of the apartment, pontificating, filling the awkward silence. She remained quiet, her eyes trained on me.

It was clear that they had both said things to each other that would be difficult to forgive — we'd all heard them. Watching me enter the stage in the middle of their war was a final stab at my mother's already wounded dreams. What she had envisioned was a happy family. In her mind, she was supposed to be a successful working mother with a loving husband. She was supposed to have 2.5 kids, a couple of nice cars, and a schedule filled with service to her community and her family. She had wanted to create a world that was different from the one she grew up in. She aimed for a picture-perfect, upwardly mobile African American home, filled with joy and love and success. She believed it was her job to have it all and do it all and be it all.

And she was failing.

My entrance into the room was a signal to her of her failure to protect me from the ugliness of the truth that was bleeding out of them both. My mother was overworked and underpaid; she was treading water in her career due to her inability or unwillingness to write in the brutal "publish or perish" world of academia. She was married to a man who seemed incapable of solvency and whose partying and drinking were a source of heartache. They had two nice cars, sure, but only one child, a child who had been virtually impossible to conceive, and whose very existence was a stain of shared lies and shame between them.

Looking back, I think my mother was trapped in the fun-house version of her dream, an upside-down reality filled with anger, fear, and resentment.

Finally, she spoke.

"Earlier," she said, wearily, almost to no one, "when I thought we were done fighting for the night, I told myself that I should go take a bath."

Then she looked at my dad, daggers for eyes.

"I thought about the gift that you gave me for my birthday," she said, "and I thought that I could put that homemade spa machine in the bottom of the tub and turn it on, and maybe just relax."

And then she turned and gazed at me, almost as though I were an apparition.

"But then I thought, *What if he throws the whole machine in the bathtub...?*"

With that she stopped, and I stood there, quietly, not wanting to imagine her dead in that water.

~~~

The next morning, as was always the case, it was as if nothing had happened. There was no discussion of the painful words that had been exchanged the night before, no reference to them at all, in fact. My mother smiled warmly at me as she prepared breakfast, and my dad slept through the early morning hours as he usually did.

A few days later, I sat at my aunt Daph's kitchen table and told her that if my parents didn't stop arguing I was going to move in with her and my cousins. And I asked her to relay that to my parents, on my behalf.

Although my ultimatum felt genuine, given I was only seven, I was unable to follow through with it. I didn't want to be dramatic (at least not in that way). I decided not to give Aunt Daph any more details about my parents' late-night battles. I became more private and withdrawn. I resolved to stay in my room at night while the dreaded internal pulse of the rhythm terrorized me to sleep. My parents' battles were minor in comparison to the one that was raging within me.

My mind and body became the enemy; I was trapped within them. I tucked away the fear and started to develop a role, a character that would stay with me: The good girl. The perfect child. The solution. It was clear that my parents had lost their ability to express their love for each other, but perhaps a shared love for me could help them find it again. Maybe my goodness could inspire a renewed tenderness between them, which would in turn create more emotional security for me, something that I so desperately needed. Perhaps there was no changing the reality that they had grown disappointed and disillusioned with each other, but I could make it better, or at least try.

After all, I was their dream come true. If their personal failures had made it impossible for them to love themselves and each other, then I would be perfect enough so that they could experience whatever love they needed through me.

CHAPTER FOUR

FROZEN

Something was happening to me at night.

Before I go any further, let me say this. I do not blame the perpetrator of this betrayal. That is not to say that I do not grapple with the effects of the betrayal itself, but, like me, he was also a scared child, struggling to make sense of the world around him. He was not an adult predator taking advantage of a younger more vulnerable girl. He was not a pedophile. The truth remains that there were things done to me—while I was sleeping, and without my consent—but the perpetrator was a child himself. It is partly my compassion for him that has kept these incidents a secret, locked in the vault of my mind.

But in choosing to not tell this story—to the adults in my life when I was a child, and publicly until now—*his* youth and innocence have been prioritized, *his* emotional vulnerabilities have been protected over my own. A long time ago, protecting his life and his story became more important than claiming mine. And in many ways, I do not regret that. Still, today, I want to protect the little boy who made those awful choices, understanding that his behavior came out of his own little-boy curiosities, pains, and struggles. In recent years, however, as I grapple with the truth of who I am, and how, and why, I have tallied the costs that his behavior had on me as a little girl, a girl with her own pains and struggles and confusion.

And I want her to have her story, too.

~~~

Sleepovers were a fixture of my upbringing. Maybe because I was an only child—or perhaps because of the communal nature of the circle of working parents who leaned on one another when busy schedules required it—for whatever reasons, there were lots of sleepovers. At my house, at my friends' houses, with cousins and with neighbors. They were always with people we knew, kids we were related to, or who lived in our community, or with whom I went to school. We were usually supervised by parents; sometimes babysitters. "Friends who were family and family who were friends," as my dad would describe them while saying grace before any meal that brought large circles together. Fun, safe, communal, and I think especially important for me, as an only child who sometimes longed for sibling-like companionship.

I remember waking up some nights with my nightgown tousled and in a peculiar arrangement. As a child, I was a wild sleeper, but I hadn't known my nightgown to ever ride up my torso and leave my chest exposed. Waking up to this level of dishevelment was disorienting. But once awake, I would be surrounded by other sleeping kids. It seemed that perhaps the trouble was imagined or created by the anxieties of my ten-year-old mind. Paranoia began to take root. And fear wreaked havoc on the night. My sleep became even more fractured, and my anxiety grew.

~~~

When I was in my thirties, I did an independent film called *The Details,* a quirky movie with a lot of raccoons, starring Tobey Maguire, Elizabeth Banks, and Ray Liotta. One afternoon, while we sat in the makeup trailer, the conversation moved toward relationships and marriage. One of the actors on set was going through a divorce, and he said something about relationships that I will never forget. He admitted to me that he had not always been fully honest in his relationships in the past. He said, "My therapist told me the cruelest thing you can ever do to another human being is to label their suspicions as false when you know them to be true." His therapist explained that when you teach a person to believe that their internal truth is a lie, you take from them the very thing that is most important to each of us—our ability to know and trust ourselves.

I have had moments in my life—more than I like to admit—where a selfish mindset has blinded me to the needs and pains of others. But in general, I am built with a sometimes codependent need to see things from another person's perspective, to understand them, to justify their feelings and their behavior and to experience their reality as my own. This is extremely useful when working to understand a character's identity and motivation, but it can be confusing when working to make sense of what happened to me.

Sometimes in daylight hours the kids in our circle of neighborhood and community friends played "house" or "husband and wife." And sometimes this role-playing involved hugging or touching—always with clothes on, and never in a way that was scary, at least not to me. But I remember one afternoon something more happened, a moment of humping and giggling and a strange sensation in my genitals that I had never felt before.

This was not abuse. In my memory, it was mutual and non-coercive behavior between curious kids. There was no pressure to play in this way. But not long after, maybe because of the strange physical pleasure that I registered, I felt guilt and shame. At some point I remember thinking that by playing house, we were doing something wrong. I don't know where the shift in perspective came from, but I remember having clear inner guidance and deciding that I did not want to play that way anymore.

Soon after, I learned from friends in the schoolyard at P.S. 182 that babies happened when husbands and wives touched each other, and I thought that because we had played house, I was going to have a baby. For months, I lived in fear that there was a human growing in my belly, but that terror dissipated when my mother coincidentally read me an age-appropriate, educational children's book about anatomy and how babies are made. I was shocked to see pictures of the male anatomy and the female anatomy, but also relieved when I realized that I had never seen an actual penis or done anything at all that was pictured in that book that would have resulted in a pregnancy. And I didn't want to.

But something was happening at night.

Again, and again, I'd have this vague sense. *What exactly was it? And who else, if anyone, was involved?*

The figure, if even real, was a mystery. His stealthy tactics and drive-by terror went unnoticed in the moment of their doing, leaving me to awaken the next day with a confusion about the scent of betrayal that lingered behind.

Two instances tipped me off. One night as I rolled over, sleep disturbed for unknown reasons, I saw a friend's body shift away from me, back under his blanket and onto his pillow, as if he was rushing to hide his awakeness. He wasn't a member of our core circle, but he was around enough that summer to earn entry to our rituals. Was he the reason that I was awake or did he, at least, know what had woken me? I whispered his name, but he didn't respond. He was entirely still, as if frozen. I said it again—nothing.

I knew he was awake. I said his name again, slightly louder this time. Another friend, lying next to us both, started to stir. I'd spoken loud enough to wake our second friend, but not the boy who continued to ignore me. Reluctantly, I rolled over and tried to go back to sleep, but I could hear the frozen boy breathing. It was the shallow breathing of a startled creature, not the deep breaths that fill the lungs of a sleeping one. As we both lay there, backs to each other less than a foot apart, I wondered why he wouldn't respond.

A few weeks later, I got a second clue.

I was asleep in bed at a neighbor's house. Her parents were out, as were mine. We were having an epic sleepover—there must have been as many as eight kids there—supervised by a "babysitter" who was in the living room watching *The Twilight Zone* with her boyfriend. I must have been in a deep slumber because when I was stirred, the light beyond my lids was too warm and bright to match the dark room that I had fallen asleep in. And as my heavy eyes slowly fluttered open, I realized that I was on my back, which was strange, because I didn't sleep on my back.

How did I get here?

I saw the light from the lamp on the bedside table flicker off.

Why had it been on?

And then I heard scrambling. I knew the frozen boy was there, but this time it seemed that maybe he was not alone. *Were there two, maybe three?* I didn't know, but I heard a muffled giggle and clambering toward the bedroom door. My covers were off, and I could feel the warm air on my uncovered limbs. My panties were pulled low—not down, but low enough to get a look at parts that are meant to be private. My nightshirt was bunched up along my clavicle.

It was clear that someone had been looking at me, maybe touching me, while I had been asleep.

"What's going on back there?" the sitter yelled from the couch in the other room. No one spoke. I struggled to wake myself up.

I clenched my covers around me and tried not to cry. I vowed to myself that I would never again allow my mind to fall that deeply into a sleep. I thought, *What just happened?* And *How could I have let it happen?*

In the morning, I was full of questions.

What had happened?

What had been done?

But I never asked the questions out loud—I was too embarrassed. I barely lifted my gaze from the ground all day. I had been trained by my parents in the light of day to ignore the horrors of the previous night. The boy seemed fine to play along. There was no acknowledgment, no apology. He seemed to believe that he had gotten out of the room quickly enough to allow himself cover and deniability. I knew something had happened, but the playing innocent, coupled with the fact that I had been only half awake, made me doubt myself. *How could I be sure?*

Plus, I thought, *if something horrible did happen to me last night, why didn't I say anything at the time? Why didn't I respond to our babysitter's inquiry? Why was I silent? Why did I wait? And what could I say now? How would I explain it all?* I didn't want to get anyone in trouble for memories of a nightmare I had no ability to prove, no language to express, and no tools to process.

At the next sleepover I was terrified; again, the frozen boy was there. I knew his chosen tactic of ignoring me, but now I wanted to confront him. I wanted to defend myself from the nightmares, real and imagined. Before bedtime, I found a quiet moment to approach him alone in a room, while he was unpacking his toothbrush and pajamas. I looked him in the eye and said his name, hoping that my simple statement of truth would invite more honesty into the moment.

"I think maybe something's happening to me," I managed to say. "At night. When I'm sleeping."

I didn't want to accuse him. I wanted to give him room to admit that he had done something terrible, something that he regretted and would promise never to do again.

Instead, he looked me dead in my face, with a confused and disgusted look on his. He shook his head and chuffed, stepped backward away from me, and then told three lies that would set the course for my greatest inner struggles going forward, lies that caused a disconnect that I would come to believe was part of the reason I have struggled for most of my life to know and trust myself.

He said, "You're crazy.

"You made that up in your head.

"I don't know what you're talking about."

And then he turned around and walked away.

～～

There were ways in which I was thought to be a golden child of our peer group. My parents both held college degrees and were believed, by the community, to be successful in their careers. My parents were (and are) still married, and regardless of the marital troubles they were having, their togetherness stood in sharp contrast to many of my friends' parents. I was materially provided for in ways that were different from lots of my friends—we had an early IBM computer and one of those printers with the paper that had tiny holes on the sides that got torn off once the images had been loudly inked. We had a dishwasher and were the first in the building to own a microwave. We had two midsize family cars and a cabin in the woods in upstate New York. On the outside, my childhood, my family, and our lives, were golden.

The socioeconomic circumstances of the frozen boy's life were more limited. Even then, and still today, I wonder if his acting out—his betrayal, both physical and psychological—was a way for him to process the distance in our given circumstances. *Was it meant to damage my spirit? Was it, consciously or not, a way for him to assert control over me in my most vulnerable hours so that he could feel more power and agency in his own life? Was this abuse a way to even the cosmic score?*

When he denied it three times—"You're crazy; you made that up in your head; I don't know what you're talking about"—something inside me shattered. I felt like the spirit within me, my self-esteem and sense of self, were under attack. But still, there was a strong, confident, free version of myself within my ten-year-old body. His denial, it seemed, was attempting to slaughter her soul. But she was determined not to go down without a fight.

The next time that we were at a sleepover under the same roof, I resolved to do whatever was needed to protect both my body and my mind. As I lay in bed, I tried to physically relax while staying mentally alert. I didn't know how long it would be, but I wanted to stay awake while pretending to be asleep, in the hopes that I would fool him into proceeding with his usual violations. Caught in the act, I imagined that he would have no choice but to admit to his crimes, and I would reclaim the truth, my truth for myself.

There were no clocks in the room, so it was impossible to know how much time had passed, but I remember beginning to get scared that the weight of my eyelids was lulling me into unconsciousness. And then, I heard it. The doorknob started to twist, slowly and with great care.

I had been living with the feeling that something was happening to me at night for so long. In this moment, it was being confirmed. He had been tiptoeing into my nightmares over and over again and knew how to best avoid discovery. The heavy wooden door slid across the carpet. I lay on my side, my back to the door. I wasn't sure that I would be able to keep the terror that was flowing through my veins from revealing itself. The small room seemed to shrink as I lay there, waiting for him to get close enough to touch me.

I had imagined this moment and had made a plan to spin around in the bed and grab his arm before he could make contact with the rest of me. But then, to my surprise, he sat down on a chair next to the bed, and I heard his body shift down into its cushions. My heart raced, but I kept my breathing slow, to match a pattern that I thought resembled sleep.

His pause was chilling. His patience broke my heart. This was not the rushed behavior of someone stumbling his way through his curiosity. This was intentional. Strategic, calculated, conscious, and controlled.

As he sat there and waited, I wondered what he was thinking. *Did he always take his time in this way before violating my body? Was this the pause he usually gave himself before breaking my trust?* I wondered if he ever thought about the consequences of his betrayal (for me, a lifetime of self-doubt and fear, disordered sleeping, disordered eating, trust issues). He knew that what he was doing was wrong, everything told me that — the quiet approach, the rushed retreats, the blatant denial, the questioning of my sanity. He knew, yet he proceeded to do it anyway. And if my suspicions were to be confirmed, he was going to try to do it now.

As I lay there, waiting to be touched, my skin crawled with fear. Guilt, dread, and sadness bubbled up from my belly, and I choked back my tears. I focused on breathing, certain that he was watching me for clues to how deeply my mind had sunken into a dream state. He had learned, maybe the hard way, that my mind needed to be completely submerged in a slumber that could mute my brain's abilities to register his abuses. He was patient in order to ensure my compliance in his private crimes, careful in his gentle brutality. *Did it scare him,* I wondered, *when I shifted in my sleep? Did he panic if my breathing changed?* Forcing myself to match his restraint with my own, I resolved to do neither, allowing my stillness to lure him.

I heard him lean forward in the chair and slowly scoot his body closer to me. I felt him put his hand on the bed next to me but not in direct contact. *Smart*, I thought. If a small movement might have woken me up, he knew, or had learned, that it was better to have me return to consciousness with his hand more innocently placed. He lifted his arm, and I felt the bed shift and knew that the next landing spot intended for that hand was me. My mind and body went into full alert.

It was true. I was not crazy. He was touching my body, repeatedly, against my will and without my consent. I swung around in the bed, my face clenched in an aspect of fierce refusal. I don't remember what I said exactly (adrenaline erased the possibility of keeping that memory), but I remember using the tone and tempo of a confident superheroine confronting her villain.

"I knew it," or "How dare you?" or "What were you thinking?"

But before I could finish talking, he fled. He knew that he'd been caught. But I was emboldened now.

I got out of bed and walked into the room where he was sleeping. There were other kids in there, too, but I didn't care.

"I'm gonna tell on you for what you did."

"No," he begged.

"I am, I'm gonna tell..."

"Please—"

I turned my back on him and began to walk through the dark hallway toward the living room where the adults were sitting. I could hear that they were watching television, and that my mother was not alone. Glasses clinked and late-night laughter between grown folks was in the air. With every step toward her, I could imagine the frozen boy's panic rising.

"Mom?" I called.

"Yes?" she called back.

Time itself froze. I took a breath, as my thoughts barreled. My legs felt weak beneath me, but my heart pounded with the strength of a warrior. I *was* a warrior—a fierce renegade who had entrapped my enemy, caught him, and defeated him.

But as I stood there silently in that hallway, with one arm on the wall to steady my dizzying perception, I did not know how to report the victory because, although the pain he inflicted was undeniable, that enemy was supposed to be my friend. I wanted to tell my mother the truth, to detail what had been happening to me. I wanted her to know that I had survived, that I was strong, that I had defended my body, my sanity, and my soul. And that he was wrong. I was not crazy.

And even though I couldn't see him, I knew that he had heard me call out to my mother, had heard her response, and that he was now waiting again, waiting to see if I would expose his crime, hoping that I would not tell the truth. I thought of him lying in that bed, imagined his soul begging for forgiveness, begging for grace. I was drenched in anger, but I didn't know what to say. Part of my fury was directed at her as well. I needed her to protect me, and she had not done that. I wanted her to scoop me up and tell me that I was OK and promise me that nothing like that would ever happen again.

I stood in that hallway, the truth caught in my throat, desperately wanting to be held by her, desperately needing to be protected from him and from this crossroads where I now stood.

But I also knew if I told her what had happened, I would be criminalizing the frozen boy. I didn't understand why he did what he did, but I knew that the punishments he might receive could negatively transform the trajectory of his life. He had made me suffer, yes, but was I now justified in inflicting suffering upon him? And would I even be believed? I had seen his denial. He was convincing. He had almost convinced me.

I decided that he would not survive me telling, and that of the two of us, I was probably the one best equipped to hold this trauma and live with the truth of it. Yes, he was the perpetrator, but I felt that he was not built to withstand the pain of facing the consequences of his actions, so I would hide my pain and cover the truth to keep him and everyone else comfortable. I had been called to journey into pain, to navigate it, metabolize it, and survive it.

That decision marked the first time I thought that it would be better to put other people's needs ahead of my own. *I'll figure it out*, I thought. *I will find my way.*

I chose to be silent. I chose to not be in truth.

I chose to continue to pretend that everything and everyone was picture perfect. The story of my haunting was now clear, but I was unwilling to tell it. I was afraid to share the horror, to reveal my pain, to be the real me. I chose the frozen boy over me, his truth over mine, because my truth would have hurt people. If there was pain to be had, I took it on for myself.

"I have a headache," I called, still standing in the hallway outside the living room. I wanted my mom to know that I was in pain, even though I had chosen not to give her the details.

"Do you want some Tylenol?" she called.

I opened my mouth to respond and took a deep breath. I wanted to say, "No, Mom, I want to be held and loved and protected by you."

But instead, I lied and said, "Yes, please."

As I heard her walk to the kitchen and ask our host to get the Tylenol, I turned on my heels and walked back to the room where he slept.

"You're welcome," I said, towering over him as if I held all the power in the world. "Don't ever do it again. Do you understand? Because, if you do, I will tell them—"

He cut me off.

"OK," he whispered. And that was that.

~~~

If I had come forward and told my parents what he had done, would I have shifted the very culture of our family and carved a pathway out of shame and silence for all of us? Would I have freed us? *Should* I have?

One of the consequences of growing up in a household with half-truths is that there is no space for trust to thrive. My parents did not trust me with their painful truths and I, in turn, learned not to trust them with mine. Not out of resentment or anger, but simply because the withholding of truth and the avoidance of pain were the unspoken rules of engagement that lived deep within the foundation of our family unit. I held my parents' hands, and together we danced as if everything was fine, knowing full well that it wasn't. I had come to understand that the best and most appropriate way to metabolize pain was to pretend that it never happened. Which is why when those demons came for me at night, I had known what song to sing, and I had abandoned myself to sing it as I stood in that hallway.

That night I learned that I was right about my hunches, but that I could never admit it, not if I wanted to keep the peace. Maintaining peace meant withholding the truth, and that void of truth was at the very center of us. Like any child looking to assign reasons to that which they could not control, I blamed that void on myself and spent my life trying to bridge it.

I stared at that gulf between my parents and me and thought that it was my job to find a way across it. I thought that perhaps if I could get to the other side I'd find the love, acceptance, and protection that I so desperately longed for and did not have the language to request.

I vowed to fill the emotional space between us so that I could feel safe, but I could not fill that space with truth. My parents' inability to express their truths modeled for me that it was inappropriate for me to express mine. Their comfort seemed to rely on pleasantries, perfectionism, and emotional isolation. And so, to be closer to them, or to move them closer to me, I chose to try to be their beautiful, perfect, gifted, quiet, and easy child. Maybe then I would be worthy—perhaps then I could finally get the fullness of their hearts.

I was scared to break the rules, to rock the boat—I knew from experience that what they preferred was a performance, and so rather than expressing my truth, I silenced my messy, raw, hurting humanness, cloaked my vulnerability in the false claim of a mild headache, and made the decision to continue to pretend and perform through life as though everything were picture-perfect.

Most especially me—I would be perfect.

But perform as I may, something in me had been awakened. I had discovered what truth could look like and feel like. I saw it in my mother's longing for freedom and in my dad's yearning for love, in the frozen boy's guilty terror and in my own clear-eyed courage. I saw it. And I wanted more of it. I needed to feel more alive and human and real. But there was, I resolved, no room for those feelings at home. If I was going to be fully human, I was going to have to do that elsewhere. I could not swim in deep waters with them—I had to do that alone.

When I woke the next morning, I could feel that something within me had changed. There were new rules in place now. They had been carved out by the decision I had made about who and what mattered most. It was not me—I was not as important as the frozen boy. I was not as important as my parents, either. I was not as important as my family, as my larger community. I was somehow, in the mind of my child self, both not as important as these people and yet wholly responsible for maintaining their goodness. I already had the tools necessary to subjugate myself and feign perfection. I had done that with my parents for years and had done it again that night.

When I had witnessed my parents' fighting, and when I caught the frozen boy in the act, these were moments of painful truth, but they were coupled with a sense of relief and power and the freedom that comes from confronting lies and standing in reality, regardless of how much it hurt.

I wanted more truth, I wanted access to the secrets that were hidden within me—the anger, the pain, the fear, the joy, the relief. I wanted it to be OK for me to be messy, to be wrong, to be bad. I couldn't feel my feelings at home; I couldn't share them with anyone. So, I set out on a journey to find places where my feelings would be accepted and my secrets could be told, even in code. I was willing to be whoever I needed to be, but I knew I had to be someone other than myself.

And this is how acting began to save my life.

~∽~

If my life as Kerry Washington was relegated to chasing safety and love through the performance of low-maintenance, good-girl perfectionism, then the characters I played became my necessary escape into messy creativity, big bold feelings, and living out loud. In every character, I got to be somebody else. And *that* person got to be a real human being—in fact, it was my job to try to make her so. Each role I took on gave me permission to escape the trappings of my family's dance and explore what being human could feel like. Each character needed me to feel deeply, to take risks, and to tell their truth.

Through acting I would meet mentors, professors, and teachers who encouraged my embodied truth—in fact, acting itself would become my mentor, whispering to me, quietly calling me to adventure. "Come play!" it would say. "Come act, come pretend." Like a seductive siren call, the scenes, the projects, the roles would call to me, saying, "forget *your* truth, tell mine instead," and as an actor I would get to explore alternate realities and step into illusions, all the while still looking for the truth in them, seeking their humanity, and searching for myself.

Looking back, I realize that in acting I discovered a lifeline that not only saved me but sustained me for decades. I have lived through my characters, looking for ways to speak freely, feel deeply, and be seen fully. To be believed. I spent years wrestling with the truth and searching for myself in every role I played, grateful for the ability to leapfrog through life under the cover of their existence.

~～～

In high school, when I was struggling emotionally, no one had to know—I could pour my heart into playing the depressed hopelessness of Ophelia and terrorizing madness of Lady Macbeth. Their big feelings could stand in for my own. Acting taught me the power of catharsis and helped me survive my own depression and madness by allowing me to express myself. Being somebody else was more comfortable for me than being me. Onstage, I knew who I was, I understood my story, and I always knew what to say and do next—it was prescribed.

Offstage, as Kerry, I was much less sure of my truth, much more insecure, confused, and lonely. The gaslighting—from the frozen boy, from my parents—had robbed me of that clarity and power.

I remember my mother asking me if I wanted to paint my room when I was in high school. As a young child, before the abuse, I had specific and very clear answers to that question—I wanted one wall that was yellow, one orange, one pink—a room according to my personal desires.

But as I got older, I lost touch with that clarity. I didn't know what colors to paint my room. I was cut off from my authenticity, too invested in what I thought I was supposed to aspire to. I landed on a palette and a look based on images torn from the Sears catalog that we used to make our Christmas lists every year. Even the wicker vanity in my room that I told myself I wanted, and the wicker chair with the peach-colored cushion—I thought I wanted them, I asked for them, I got them, but I never used them.

In high school I would float between a lot of different social groups. I hung out with members of the choir, theater kids, students of color, white kids. I noticed that I couldn't avoid taking on the social mores of whatever group I was with at any given moment. I was looking to belong; I needed to fit in. Back then, without a deeper understanding of who I was, there was a desperation to the shape-shifting. Even with boyfriends, I would disappear into their lives, their worlds, their families, looking to ground myself in whatever details would make me undeniably belong to them.

Even today, there is the inevitable code-switching and double consciousness required for survival as a Black person in America, but that shape-shifting can be empowering. As an adult, I've told myself that I was not abandoning myself to fit in—I was flexing my capacity to feel at home in diverse environments. But if I'm honest, it's not until recently that I've begun to understand how to be an integrated person who moves fluidly through different spaces as herself.

After the abuse, when my mother asked me what color I wanted for the walls of my room, I didn't know, because I didn't have a favorite color. Lady Macbeth did; Ophelia did. I knew exactly how they spoke, what they wanted to wear, and how they would furnish their homes in their imaginary lives onstage.

But in my own home, when it came to Kerry's thoughts and desires, something in me had frozen over.

CHAPTER FIVE

AGENCY

When I first started auditioning professionally, I was thirteen years old and a student at the Spence School, an exclusive all-girls college preparatory school on Manhattan's Upper East Side. Founded in 1892, the school is world-renowned for creating an environment of intellectual curiosity and rigor for the daughters of New York's wealthiest and most privileged families. And occasionally, somebody like me, from the Bronx.

The commute from our apartment to the trademark red doors that signal the threshold into Spence took about an hour. Each day, often before the sun rose, I would wait to board the Bx36 bus at the corner of Pugsley and Randall Avenues or run from the entryway of my building to catch it. Once on, I would flash my half-fare bus pass and begin the ride toward the elevated subway station in Parkchester's Hugh J. Grant Circle. (This was where I caught the same number 6 train Jennifer

Lopez would later name an album after, because this was the stop closest to her childhood home, too.)

Parkchester was the end of the line for the local 6. When I was twelve years old, the night before I had to make my first commute into Manhattan, my mother did a practice run with me, hopping from bus to train and then walking from the Eighty-Sixth Street station, west for two and a half long avenue blocks, and then north for five streets, to 22 East Ninety-First Street, where I would spend the majority of my time for the next six years of my life.

Before touring Spence, and other New York City independent schools, it would have been impossible for me to imagine the culture of affluence and entitlement that existed both inside these academic institutions and in the lives of the people who patronized them. The wealth of many of these families and the opportunities that it afforded them was shocking. I found myself trying to make sense of the massive inequity that I witnessed and traveled through from one end of my commute to the other. I had dealt with a level of disorientation and othering when the Talented and Gifted program moved to the mostly Italian American North Bronx. But even while race and ethnicity set me apart from those peers, we were fundamentally still a bunch of kids from the Bronx, whose grandparents had sailed into Ellis Island decades earlier with the hopes of building a better life for themselves in the United States. My grandparents came burdened with the additional challenges of a caste system born of the history of slavery in the Caribbean, but we were still mostly members of the same second-generation American middle class—albeit some of us upper middle class and some of us more working middle class. What I witnessed at Spence was an entirely new universe unto itself.

At Pugsley Avenue, our apartment was one of ten on the twelfth floor. To arrive at 12D required a long walk down a hallway lit from above with unforgiving fluorescent fixtures. In contrast, I will never forget the first time I stood in the elevator of a large doorman building on Fifth Avenue and had the doors slide open into a grand apartment that took up the entire floor. At first, I felt bewildered—*How could this be?* Then betrayed: *How did I not know it was even possible to live like this?* Then resentful: *Why don't I know anyone who lives like this?* And finally, enraged: *Why does it seem that no one who lives like this looks like me?* But even then, I knew to hide this cocktail of emotions from the people on the other side of the elevator door. Showing those feelings would have signaled to my schoolmates that I was not accustomed to the riches that defined their daily existence and would have further outed me as "other." Not every one of my classmates was extremely wealthy, but even given the slight economic diversity within the student body, the school itself was an exercise in privilege and plentitude.

For starters, there was no cafeteria at Spence; there was only a dining room. And in that dining room, there was no Styrofoam to be found and not a spork in sight. The young ladies at Spence ate every single meal of every single school day with silverware and china. The school had a ceramics studio and a photography lab, an underground fitness facility, an elegant library engulfed in rich dark carpentry, and state-of-the-art classrooms with the most modern technology.

As one might imagine, this kind of education was tremendously expensive. And while I was afforded both financial aid and a partial academic scholarship, the remainder, which my parents still had to scrape together, was a weight not easy to bear.

In the eighth grade, when I was in my second year at Spence, the administrative assistant to the head of Middle School was Holly Schenk. Ms. Schenk — or Holly, as we were able to affectionately call her once we had left Middle School for Upper School — had an office directly across from the elevator on the fifth floor, where seventh- and eighth-grade lockers held the sweat, tears, and dreams of hardworking girls on the verge of becoming women. When Holly welcomed you to the hallways, her high-pitched, sugary-sweet tones spread smiles across that fifth floor. Confessions in her presence seemed inevitable; she was devastatingly easy to talk to.

As a twelve-year-old facing the tremendous culture clash of the world I lived in versus the one where I was educated, kicking off my discounted boat shoes (bought at an outlet mall in upstate New York) and sitting cross-legged in the chair beside Holly's desk made me feel like there was a small spot of safety in this vast unknown land. I felt close to Holly. She did not know everything about me — she, too, got an edited version, carefully crafted to meet the expectations of my audience — but she knew how much I loved to act. In my first year at Spence, I had been cast in the role of the little sister in a production that was part of the Upper School season. Then, toward the end of seventh grade, I would audition for and be invited to join TADA!, an esteemed children's theater troupe in New York. Although this was not a paid gig, in many ways it was my first taste of artistic professionalism. Our rehearsal and performance schedules were rigorous, and we were held to a high standard of responsibility—for example, as kids, we were taught and expected to take written notes at the end of each rehearsal and show and to adjust our performances based on them.

In eighth grade, I would be cast as a fairy in the Upper School's production of *A Midsummer Night's Dream* because Mr. Coleman, our director, had chosen to source his fairies from the younger grades. Even in those early years, the art of becoming other people (and the joy and solace that it brought me) had become part of who I was and how I was seen at Spence. This production, incidentally, is the only time I have had the delight of working alongside another Spence girl, Gwyneth Paltrow, who was cast in the role of Queen Titania.

Holly said that her friend Juliet Taylor, a casting director, was having a tough time filling the role of a young Black woman in an upcoming blockbuster film based on the bestselling novel *Interview with the Vampire*. None of the industry language made sense to me, but sitting at Holly's desk listening to her, it was clear that this was an exciting prospect, an opportunity, perhaps, to play in the big leagues. I was performing with a children's theater company and in school plays, but I had never been in a real professional casting office for film, never mind the office of a legend, the woman responsible for casting films like *Network* and *Mississippi Burning*. But I did not know what I did not know.

So, for the first time in my life, I held script "sides" in my hands (Holly had printed them for me), and I practiced the lines over and over again. I didn't quite know what to expect while auditioning for a major motion picture, but I prepared with all the tools I'd gathered and set out to hopefully not embarrass my friend Holly after she had so generously recommended me for the role.

I remember walking into Juliet Taylor's office and seeing posters for movies that we loved as a family — *Close Encounters of the Third Kind* was a particular favorite of my dad's — and realizing that this woman, Juliet, and her partner, Ellen Lewis, were dream weavers. They were the people who decided who got to do what I loved to do most. I felt like I had just entered Oz. I sat down but felt my nervous energy rising within me and almost immediately bounced back up and asked the associate in the waiting area for a bathroom. She handed me a key and directed me down the hallway. By the time I came back, Juliet was ready.

Juliet's office revealed more posters of more films with more actors whom I admired and loved. We shared some small talk about where we were from, and about our mutual friend, Holly, and about Spence, and I could feel that there was extra warmth in the room based on those two associations. To Juliet, I may have been a Black girl from the Bronx, but I was also attending one of the most elite educational institutions in the country and had been preapproved by her Upper East Side girlfriend of decades. These details earned me goodwill in the unfair game of access and privilege. There was the feeling in the room that although I was not exactly one of them, I was a reasonably exceptional delight, a properly trained and comfortably adjacent novelty.

Juliet turned on a camcorder in the back of the room and began to read the scene with me. I took a deep breath and invited my imagination to sink into an alternate reality of blood and lust, vampires and queens.

When I finished, I was met with Juliet's quizzical gaze.

"Who's your agent?" she said.

"I don't have one," I replied, barely sure of what that was or what it meant.

"Interesting," she said. And then it was clear that the audition was done. I left the room feeling inspired by this brush with eminence and eager to find a way to get back to it.

The following day at school, Holly greeted me with a smile and a hug.

"You were magnificent," she said. "Unfortunately, Juliet does not think that this is the right role for you." My heart dropped. "She said that you might be too young for it, but she thought you were wonderful, and she wants to help you get an agent!"

Feeling mostly disappointed and rejected at the time, I had no idea the pot of gold that I had stumbled upon. Juliet had given Holly the names of the top five talent agencies representing kids in New York. She referenced exactly whom to call within each company and said that she would personally call each of them ahead of time to ensure that they would set a meeting with me.

Years later I would learn about the enormous difficulties that actors faced in procuring agent representation, and I would marvel at the miraculous luck I'd been afforded. I never had to send out hundreds of mailers, or make hours of cold calls, or perform in dozens of showcases in an effort to meet with an agent, as so many actors do. Juliet Taylor had gifted me the golden ticket; I was learning what privilege looked like.

The first agency on the list was J. Michael Bloom. In terms of "kids"—meaning everyone from babies to twentysomething actors with baby faces—Bloom had some of the hottest young talent at the time on its roster: Marlon Wayans (then still a student at LaGuardia High School of Music & Art and Performing Arts), Ethan Hawke, Winona Ryder, even Lauryn Hill.

~~

When I was graduating elementary school and interviewing at all the best independent schools in New York, my cousin Michael, who attended University of Pennsylvania and understood the shoulders I was about to rub, gave me advice that would stick with me. I often thought of it when I felt pressured to impress holders of power so that I could gain acceptance into their realm.

"Listen," Michael had said, rifling through the wallet he had just been given that Christmas because he hoped that it would come with money inside, something that apparently wealthy parents did when they gave wallets to their kids. (There was no money inside.) "Always remember that you are interviewing them as much as they are interviewing you. Ask them a question, a question that makes them feel like you may want to choose another school instead. Say 'What distinguishes your school from some of the other institutions I'm visiting? Why should I choose this school over some of the other great independent schools?'"

My mother and I arrived at the building where J. Michael Bloom kept their offices. I remember seeing a larger-than-life sculpture in the lobby, signaling to me that these were professional people with money to burn.

That afternoon, I sat in the bullpen offices of J. Michael Bloom and met with agents in both the commercial and legit (meaning film, television, theater) divisions of the company. I had already performed a monologue for them, and they had given me "cold sides" to read (lines for a scene that I had to prepare on the spot). Then it was time to talk. I presented them with Michael's questions. Just as those questions had wooed and wowed the administrators at all the independent school interviews, here, too, they would make the agents justify their value instead of begging them to see mine. The deal was further sealed when they mentioned an audition later that week that I would be "perfect" for. I pulled out my day planner (not to impress them, but because it was a mandatory organizational item at Spence), and the team of agents looked at me as if I were an apparition of maturity in a landscape of juvenile chaos.

This was the big leagues. I agreed to sign a three-year contract with the agency before leaving the building. My mother had heard that we should never work with an agency that "makes money before you do." The fact that J. Michael Bloom worked on commission, and that their rate of commission was in line with industry standards, made us confident that we were not being conned.

I never made it to the other four agencies. There was no need. The agents at J. Michael Bloom thought I was wonderful, and I fooled them into thinking that I thought I was wonderful, too.

On the drive home, back up to the Bronx, I studied my mother's pensive face and thought that maybe she was trying to predict how this new chapter of my life would unfold and all the potential dangers that lay ahead.

"You can audition only as long as it does not affect your grades," she said, hesitatingly. She seemed to be testing out how these new rules felt to her. "And if you want to take this on, it has to be your responsibility completely. You have to write down the appointments, you have to take the subway to the auditions, and you have to prepare on your own."

I wondered whether my mother was creating distance between herself and what she saw as a dangerous path forward, or if she was just asserting limitations to keep me focused on the things that mattered most to her. Maybe she was trying to warn me that this was a space in which she had little wisdom and experience to share, or maybe she was just using the moment as a teaching opportunity. But regardless of what she said, or why, what I heard most was that I now had permission to try to be a professional actor.

The trying, however, was a lot less fun and exciting than I thought it would be. Auditioning professionally was terrifying. The process of being scrutinized and evaluated and then often dismissed—sometimes instantaneously, as in commercial auditions—was profoundly intimidating. Every time I had a "go see," I would rush after school to change out of my Upper East Side all-girls school uniform into whatever outfit I thought might get me the job as America's most likeable new teenager. Because my mother did not want me to miss school for auditions, after a long day of classes I would hustle to take the subway farther downtown, even farther away from our apartment in the Bronx. I nervously hurried through buildings filled with offices—a design studio, a shipping company, a security firm, a temp agency, all animated by the organized chaos of adults at work—until I found the location I was looking for: a casting office. There, I would pour my heart into delivering dialogue designed to entertain my fellow teenagers in after-school specials, or into marketing copy meant to utilize my charisma to sell soap. Or tampons. Or potato chips. Or the newest electronic gadget that we were all supposed to want.

Initially, acting was a place where I felt safe. Now, in the pursuit of professional success, my love for acting was becoming tainted.

I hadn't started to audition professionally with the goal of making money, but financial success quickly became the driving force. Sensing my parents' worry without understanding where it was coming from, I felt, again, that it was up to me to do better. Under the spotlight of the auditioning process, my people-pleasing and perfectionism mushroomed exponentially. I needed all those people on the other side of the audition table to like me — the directors, casting directors, producers, everyone. I wanted to book the job, but not just for the reward to my ego. I was sensing continued economic strain from my parents, and I thought it was my job to fix it. After all, wasn't Spence their biggest financial burden?

The seduction of monetary reward had put blood in the water that my mother couldn't resist sniffing out. And the more my mother interrogated me, with a veneer of concern, about why I wasn't booking work, the more frightened I became. I brought that terror into auditions, where casting directors dismissed me before I even opened my mouth. This in turn created more fear and insecurity and fewer job opportunities.

I cannot say exactly when she started to realize that my hobby could contribute to our household, but I remember one day stepping off the elevator in Building Four with my mother walking just ahead of me. She was opening envelopes and reviewing bills. With an exasperated sigh, she glanced over her shoulder to ask, "What's been going on with these auditions? You haven't booked a job in some time...."

My diaphragm locked up. My ears started to burn. *Was she tallying my losses? Studying my inadequacies?* My mother was pointing out my failures to me and asking me why I wasn't better able to provide. My heart filled with shame and guilt. What was, for my mother, probably just a passing inquiry formed out of momentary frustration became a torturously obsessive thought for me.

What am *I doing wrong?* I asked myself. *Why haven't I booked any acting jobs?* I knew that even just one professional acting gig could have provided some relief for my family, relief from the bills that she was rifling through as we walked down the hallway. So why hadn't I been able to be more perfect? Why didn't people want me in their projects and on their screens? Was I not pretty enough, sexy enough, thin enough? These questions made me think that I had to transform myself to do better and *be* better. I started to resent my parents for the pressure I felt to book. And I started to hate auditions, exactly when I needed the work the most.

~~~

Until acting became a feasible source of income, my mother was reluctant for me to choose the arts as a profession. Even though they donated small amounts to PBS every year and took me to museums and concerts and discounted Broadway shows, my mother would always still say "Don't be an actor, be a lawyer for actors. Closing arguments are basically monologues." Although she never missed a school concert or play, she was terrified that in the pursuit of professional artistry, I would starve. In her mind, there was no solid, secure pathway for success. And the odds were most definitely not in my favor.

We didn't know any famous people except for Jennifer Lopez, who, though older than me, attended the same Boys & Girls Club. But Jennifer was different — even when she was a kid in the neighborhood, we all knew that she was the kind of magnetic and gorgeous person who becomes a cultural icon. (I did not think I was either of those things, so I didn't envision that kind of future for myself.) My parents didn't know any actors who'd "made it" — the sheer statistical improbability of it was probably also in the back of my mother's mind when she worried about my professional prospects.

But even though it wasn't on the big or small screen, I found my way to an acting job that sustained me, on and off, for close to a decade. The gig didn't offer the kind of pay that transformed the economic realities of our home. But it did provide me with spending money that allowed me to feel like less of a disappointment and burden.

When I was twelve, my mother saw an ad for an audition with a theater company based out of Mount Sinai Hospital's Adolescent Health Center in New York City — the S.T.A.R. Program (Serving Teens through Arts Resources). It was 1989, a few years into the AIDS epidemic. This theater company traveled around the tristate area doing peer-to-peer theatrical performances to educate young people on safer sex practices, with the goal of mitigating the spread of HIV.

The shows, which were written and performed by the young members of the company, dealt with issues like self-esteem, loss of virginity, safer sex, homosexuality, drug abuse, and living with family members who are HIV positive. To perform in the company, we had to undergo training to become peer educators and adolescent health experts. We wrote the skits and the music and choreographed the dance routines—we'd tailor each performance to the age of the students and the particular issues most relevant to their community. We'd often change the sketches to include local references that helped connect us to our audience. And we became an award-winning, highly regarded national model for theater in education.

Every Sunday, we would meet in a gym on the eighth floor of Mount Sinai Hospital to rehearse from 10 a.m. to 4 p.m. Six intense hours of writing, acting, singing, dancing, improvisation, theater games, and educational workshops. It was an intellectual and creative paradise. When I joined S.T.A.R. theater, I was the youngest person in the company. But through this circle of artists, I discovered a trusted community of peers who provided me with my first experience of the power of found family. I learned how to be in my body, and to be in my truth as Kerry, in this small pocket of creative community. And it was phenomenal acting training, too.

S.T.A.R. theater often performed for hostage audiences. Many of the young people who saw our show had not chosen to attend the performance. Instead, they had been shuffled into an auditorium (or gymnasium or cafeteria or lobby) by a teacher or guidance counselor. To capture and hold the attention of a resistant crowd—who would sometimes shout things at us as we performed to distract or derail us or maybe just impress their friends—was sometimes exhausting. But it seeded within us a tenacity and fearlessness as performers that

I know has served me throughout my career. And the sense of victory that comes from winning over a reluctant audience — making them laugh, cry, and dance along at the end of a show — supersedes any feeling I have ever had onstage, even including a standing ovation on Broadway.

The other reason why my years spent working with S.T.A.R. were so pivotal in my development as an actor was that for almost every show we stayed in character afterward to do an interactive "talkback" with audiences. There, we would speak with them directly as the characters we were playing and about the challenges "we" were facing. All the vignettes in the show were open-ended, so within each scene we would present a problem and then, after the performance, ask the audience for advice. We were basically doing improv with as many as three hundred audience members at a time. To do this effectively, each actor in the company had to build a deep and thorough backstory for their character, filling out every detail of their existence and memorizing it thoroughly, so that they could respond to an audience member with both spontaneity and clarity. We had to know our characters inside and out so that our reactions to the audience felt true and real. And following the tenets of improvisation, we strove to say "yes, and" — to be receptive to whatever an audience member said, answer all their questions, remain nimble, and most of all, be generous. And the stakes were magnified because with each performance, these teenagers were facing the same life and death decisions that had been written into the show. Making them believe that the characters were real was the exact wizardry we had to master to gain their trust and offer tools for better communication and decision-making that could save their lives.

This is when the connection between art and social change became crystal clear to me. I started to understand the power of representation, the need for people to see themselves in the content they consume, but also the power of content to change how they think and feel and behave. When our ability to connect authentically with our audiences was challenged—because a church didn't want us to mention homosexuality, or a school board was resistant to us using the word "condom"—our devotion to the material, in service of our audience, propelled us into activism. It wasn't just what we were saying in the show that made us educators and activists. It was also how we protected the art we were making, how we defended it, how we fought for the right to have it live in the world.

This work—as an artist, as an educator, and as an activist—helped me join a community of changemakers. I started attending rallies and speaking at conferences, meeting with public officials, and talking about these issues in the press. As I began to work more and more as a professional actor, I found myself drawn to art that was rooted in activism—like working with V (formerly known as Eve Ensler) and her organization, V-Day, to develop and perform material aimed at ending violence against women—as well as work that, though not explicitly educational, still allowed audiences to connect with bold, honest, authentic representations of themselves. I wanted to play complicated characters with difficult truths; I wanted to never be afraid if the stakes were high and if the material was controversial. I vowed to value my identity as both an artist and activist throughout my career, wherever it took me.

~~~

While I was working with S.T.A.R, Peter Jennings, then the beloved host of ABC's *World News Tonight,* aired a primetime special on the AIDS epidemic featuring teens talking about sex and AIDS. As part of a group of peer educators, I was invited to come and talk to the producers about what issues should be discussed on the show. In the meeting, I wound up performing a monologue from our S.T.A.R. repertoire, and the producers were blown away. "You're going to do that on the special," they said. "Live."

I mostly tried to keep my sex education life separate from my prep school world, but I was still known as the Condom Lady at Spence—everybody knew if you needed condoms, you should contact Kerry (I always carried an assortment of rainbow-colored condoms that I'd gotten from the Adolescent Health Center in my backpack). The day after the special aired, I walked into rehearsal at our brother school, Collegiate (I was playing Lady Macbeth). Our director, one of their drama teachers, had seen the special and was full of praise for the monologue.

"Thank you," I said, trying to deflect. "I've been doing that monologue for a long time."

"What interested me most," he said, "was the moment after the monologue ended — I watched you come out of the flow and back into yourself."

"What do you mean?" I said.

"Go back and watch it."

My parents had recorded it on our VCR, and when I rewatched it, I saw exactly what he meant: I witnessed what entry into and exit from flow looked like for me. I saw myself drop into the alternate reality of this character, as if a switch had been flipped and the train of my identity was now flying down a different track. And then, when the monologue was over, I pulled myself back into consciousness. I saw myself return to reality, reembodied as Kerry. The room filled with applause as I sat back in my chair, exhausted and wrung out.

It's no accident that my director made the observation about that performance while I was rehearsing to play Lady Macbeth. In that play, she calls upon spirits to transform her reality. What I saw when I watched the monologue was almost like a conjuring. Even though I didn't yet know how to fully control it, I knew that when I could plug into the character and give myself over to the reality of the performance, what happened felt like sorcery and was perceived as magic.

CHAPTER SIX

A NEW YOU

I t was my first crime.

~~~

I was a wanted child, five years in the trying, but even before I knew the timeline, I knew deep in my core how much I mattered to my parents, how loved I was, how longed for I had been. I sensed from an early age that the gift of life they had bestowed upon me came with enormous expectations. And as the Bible says: "To whom much is given, much is expected."

I was their daughter, and I was assigned the task of fulfilling that role enthusiastically. It wasn't always clear how to meet those expectations or live up to them, but I found myself constantly trying to do so. I wanted to be the best version of myself, better each day than the day before, because a part of me knew, even subconsciously, that while I was their everything, my parents were holding me at arm's length. I felt that they did not trust me to know them fully. And I was convinced that I simply was not good enough to earn their love and trust. If I had been good enough, my parents would have been able to love me more honestly, freely, and intimately, right?

One day after school, as I roamed the aisles of the Pelham Bay Library, looking for imaginary worlds to escape into, I stumbled upon a book called *A New You*. Its title lurched toward me and offered a balm for the wounds of my insecurities. The full title of the book was *A New You: The Art of Good Grooming*, and it was an illustrated textbook of etiquette guidelines aimed at young women. It detailed advice on everything from manners to nutrition, to skin care, to exercise. It was published in the mid-sixties, and I was obsessed with it. I checked it out of the library and read it cover to cover, devouring every tidbit of insight, digesting every piece of advice. I studied the book, slept with it, turned to it again and again, day after day. I was looking for how to become a better me, the best me possible. I was certain that self-improvement would make it possible for my parents to fully connect with me, and that then I would be deserving of full-minded attention and full-hearted love. I wanted the book to make me better so that my world would feel safer. I thought the book could allow me that control, that my perfection could heal our family's disconnection.

And so, I kept that book. I did not return *A New You* on its due date, or the next one, or the one after that. I never returned that book. I have no idea what fines I incurred. I would have paid them—I would have given anything to keep that bound atlas of self-improvement, but I never dared to bring the book back to the library. Withholding it became my first crime. I was determined to never give up on being someone other than me, someone better.

Being me was uncomfortable. More often than not, I felt unsteady. I had the vague notion that something was wrong, that there were secrets, and that maybe something about me was unacceptable or unlovable.

This culture of secrecy resulted in two dueling frameworks that shaped my sense of self and my relationship to the world. The first was one of self-reliance, in which I believed that I was on my own. I felt that it was impossible to be fully honest and fully myself with anyone. The second framework was the belief that I didn't have the emotional maturity to understand the complexity of my own truth. I knew that there were things they weren't telling me, things that they thought I couldn't handle. I interpreted my parents' lack of transparency as a clear message that I was unable to deal with the realities of life.

I did not reach for connections that were real and true; instead, I wanted to perform and escape into the hidden canyons of my imagination. And when life required me to exist in the realm of reality, I found ways to perform still, reaching for facades of lovable perfection and pursuing the freedom that I thought might be granted to me if only I could unlock the secrets of how to be, or maybe even just pretend to be, better.

~~~

When I was eleven, I was walking along Pugsley Avenue with a neighborhood friend, Nicole, on our way to our local supermarket, Key Food. I wouldn't have been allowed to go by myself, but Nicole was four years older than me and there was safety in numbers—even if the number was just two. I was wearing a necklace that I'd recently gotten as a gift for my sixth-grade graduation, a pendant in the shape of the Greek symbol for theater—with one mask representing comedy, and the other representing tragedy. I had seen it months before while shopping with my mother and had fallen in love with those two tiny masks. I wanted the pendant because I felt that it communicated to the world what I was most passionate about. I had a painted ceramic version of the masks that hung on my bedroom wall, too. The image of one face smiling and the other in tears held deeper meaning for me, not only as a symbol of my favorite hobby, but also as a representation of both the masks I was learning to wear in life to hide my true feelings and the emotional fluency I was allowed to experience onstage.

As we walked back with the groceries, a group of older boys—about five of them, ranging in age from about fourteen to sixteen—saw us, crossed the street, came up behind us, and asked us if we had any money.

Our denials were met with incredulity.

"We know you have money cuz you just came from the grocery store—you didn't spend all of it . . . ." And with that, one of the boys ripped my necklace off my neck and Nicole's earrings out of her ears, causing one of her lobes to bleed.

"If you don't scream, we won't hurt you," one of them said.

I was terrified. The sidewalks were empty, but I could see my building in the distance. The boys surrounded us with a kind of fight-stance shuffle — their guard was up, their adrenaline racing. I wanted to disappear. I was amazed that Nicole held tight to the small bag of groceries, but it was clear that food was not what they were hungry for. I watched these young men make eye contact with each other, our gold jewelry in their hands. They seemed to agree that the robbery was complete, and with that, they took off running. Nicole and I ran home, too.

We didn't call the police — that was rarely the first response to a crisis or danger when growing up in the Bronx. But we did tell our moms. Later, my dad got home from work and went out looking for the boys, but his search was futile and perhaps meant mostly to express his deep care, or perhaps as a way to release his frustration that there wasn't more that he could do.

The necklace was gone. My masks were stolen from me, likely already sold to a pawnshop or melted down into an untraceable ball of gold, ready to be formed into someone else's dream.

I refused to wear a necklace for years after that.

~~~

In addition to living a few floors below me at 630 Pugsley Avenue, Nicole was also a member of TADA! Her mom, Hilma, was seldom home in the afternoons because she worked long shifts as a nurse. As members of the company, we used to hang out together, and one day I got permission to invite a bunch of kids over. The deal with my parents was that I was allowed to invite my friends, but we had to come straight to apartment 12D, avoiding unsupervised time hanging out in the streets.

Longing for more freedom and autonomy, and wanting to spend at least some time away from the watchful eyes of my mother, we decided to go to Nicole's apartment first and hang out without parental supervision. I can't fully remember what we did there—in other kids' homes we sometimes smoked cigarettes or giggled while watching somebody's father's porn—but I am pretty sure that neither of those things happened that afternoon. We mostly just sat around and laughed and talked without a guardian. But unfortunately for me, one of the windows in my parents' apartment faced the bus stop at the corner where the Bx36 bus dropped us off. My mother saw us getting off the bus . . . and then waited patiently until I finally came home.

"Where were you?" she said, feigning ignorance, when I came through the door.

"We just came straight home," I said. "The bus just got here. . . ."

She looked away from me.

"Do you wanna try to answer that again?" she said.

I was caught. I looked at her and saw the disappointment in her eyes. There was no veil between us; I had let her down. I thought I was playing by the rules. I thought that in our family we protected each other from painful truths. I knew that she and my dad kept secrets—from me and from each other. But now I was feeling guilty for participating in a culture they had built. I had gotten caught in a lie, and that truth broke her heart.

After that, I was determined to never disappoint my mother again. I would still lie, yes, but I resolved to never get caught. I became a much better liar, more calculating, more convincing, more immersive. I built entire imaginative worlds around my lies and refined my pretend identity as an innocent good girl who followed the rules.

This would prove to be a crucial skill, because by fifteen, there was so much more to lie about. There were boyfriends, and parties, and drugs, and alcohol, and I was heading out to clubs in New York City, even on school nights. Soul Kitchen — my favorite party of the week — was every Monday night and lasted long into the wee hours. My drink of choice was a whiskey sour, which marketed itself as mature and strong but was mostly sweet, fast-acting, and easy to drink. Often, we arrived at statistics class hungover and exhausted each Tuesday at 8:20 a.m.

Suddenly, I was using alcohol, and sometimes food, and sometimes weed, and sometimes sex, to alter my brain chemistry and allow me a dangerously destructive escape. During the daytime I was the model adolescent, imparting my wisdom and peer education to teenagers all over the city, participating in student government and other extracurricular activities, and bringing home solid grades.

But at night, I was playing a different role, a messier one. I was pushing up against the boundaries of what was expected of me, searching for a deeper sense of where the performance ended and the real me began. I was lying, drinking, and partying like a character in one of our S.T.A.R. theater vignettes, but unlike those characters, I didn't need an audience to fix me—my perfectionism and people-pleasing skills allowed me to maintain a facade and remain high-functioning.

Everything was FINE.

～～

"Hey, Dad, we're back at Ella's place," I said, pretending we'd made it to my friend's apartment.

A bunch of us were at a diner on the corner of First Avenue and Twenty-Third Street. Ella was a girl in our circle whose parents were often away, and we were headed to her apartment on the East River. It was late, but I knew enough to call my dad from a pay phone in the diner entryway.

What I could have said was, "Hey, Dad, I know it's curfew, but we're really hungry. Can we go out to a diner?" But that would have been the truth. This was not the culture of my family—the culture of my family was lie, pretend, make it OK.

"So, if I hang up the phone and I call you back, you'll be at Ella's, right?" he said.

"Yeah, Dad," I said, feigning annoyance that he wasn't trusting me. "I mean, you'll probably wake up her mom, but go ahead."

"OK, kid," he said.

We hung up. I walked back to the table, sat back down with my girlfriends, and said, "Either I just got away with the greatest lie of our teenage years, or I'm dead and we're fucked."

(He never called Ella's apartment.)

The lying became a way of life for me. And when I wasn't lying, I was positioning the truth in a way that was most acceptable to others—especially when it came to my parents. When facing challenges, or making enormous decisions, I rarely shared them with my dad, and usually only told my mother after the fact. For example, I was in my junior year of high school when I lost my virginity. It had been a huge decision at the time, but I presented it to my mother as though it hadn't yet happened. I didn't want her to know that I'd been lying to her; I purported innocence and pretended to seek her counsel. I shared all the reasons why I thought it was a good idea, but none of the emotional vulnerability that the decision had entailed.

Similarly, when in my adolescent years I had an ongoing romantic relationship with a girl, my mother asked casually, "What's going on with you two?"

But I called her bluff.

"Do you really wanna know?" I said, hoping that she didn't. Banking on it, in fact.

"No," she said.

The conversation was now in my hands.

"We're close," I said, trying to make light of the withholding.

"OK," she said, seemingly relieved to be spared the details.

I thought that I was taking care of them, parsing out the truth in ways they could handle, because that's what I thought they were doing to me.

When I looked in my mother's eyes and saw the veil between us, I never thought, *My mother's keeping a secret from me—she's maintaining this distance because it keeps her safe.* Instead, I thought, *Why do I feel like I have to lie to them all the time? What's wrong with me that my parents can't let me in?*

~∽~

One Sunday evening, during one of our holiday breaks in S.T.A.R., my mom, dad, and I were walking the path from the parking lot to the back door of Building Four of Jamie Towers. As usual, the walk up the path was accompanied by the jangle of my parents' keys. There were keys to the car, keys to the building, keys to the apartment, keys to our cabin and its nearby shed, keys to their work offices, mailbox keys. Once the back door was unlocked, my mother—ever the family administrator—would continue walking past the elevators and toward the banks of mailboxes in the front lobby, while my dad pressed the button calling the elevator to come down and retrieve us.

Inside the elevator, we rode together quietly while my mother looked through the mail. The elevators at Jamie Towers were small. In rush hour, it would not be uncommon to have neighbors squeezed tightly together, heading downstairs to catch buses or unlicensed cabs or begin their drives to work. The walls of the elevator were covered in strange wood-like plastic tiles of geometrical patterns covered in a heavy gloss, which was meant to retain a shine but instead invited kids in the building—including friends of mine—to carve their initials into its layers, the way I imagine kids in a different landscape might carve their initials onto a tree. Layered over the etchings were "tags" drawn with permanent markers. It would be decades before museums all over the world would celebrate Bronx graffiti and academics would defend it, but for now it was evidence of a building that had lost control of its young people and was unable to maintain its decorum.

But none of the tags were mine. At fourteen years old, I was still the good girl, determined to play by the rules to win approval and acceptance. I would have no more tagged an elevator than jumped over the moon. Still, I was a teenager; spending endless hours with my parents was not a favorite pastime, and extended conversations with them even less so. While I stared at the floor of the elevator, out of the corner of my eye I could feel my mother's breath pause as she came across an envelope that made her stop flipping through the mail. My dad noticed it, too, and he turned to face her with an expression that asked, "What?"

"Worthbern sent us a Christmas card," she said dryly, knowing that her husband would read between the lines and understand the irony. Dad chuckled softly and looked away from her toward the same floor that I was staring at.

"Who's Worthbern?" I asked, glancing upward.

But my question was met with a wall of silence that suggested I had morphed into invisibility. My parents didn't look at me—their reaction was to simply pretend that nothing had been said. They stood in the small elevator with me, in complete silence, ignoring not just my question but me. And when the elevator door opened onto the fluorescent lights of the twelfth floor, we exited in that continued silence until a new subject was broached, and Worthbern was forgotten.

The name was forgotten by me, in fact, for years. The next time I heard it, I was sitting on the king-size bed that took up most of my parents' bedroom. I was home visiting from college and had been summoned by my parents to their room for "a talk." It was nighttime, and the warm glow from the lamp on my dad's dresser created shadows within the creases of the remorse on his face. And while I was no stranger to lengthy speeches from my dad, from his posture I could tell that the tone of this talk would be different.

"Sit down, kid," he said. I perched myself on the edge of the mattress, uncomfortable in the center of it.

"I have always been proud of the fact that I do not have a record...," he said.

Due to the biases of the justice system against African American men, the absence of a criminal record among the men in my father's family was rare. He had taken pride in being a statistical anomaly.

"So, it's hard for me to share this with you," he went on.

I was concerned, but also intrigued. I wondered if the details I was about to hear were going to provide some clarity, as if a fog might be lifted.

What followed was a detailed account of an IRS investigation involving real estate, drug dealers, and tax evasion.

My dad was in trouble. And he was pleading guilty. He and my mother had wanted to keep this entire ordeal a secret from me — the investigation, their legal battles, and my dad's eventual admission of guilt. But their lawyer, Worthbern, hoped that if I wrote to the judge, defending my dad and detailing the emotional suffering he had already endured, it would help lighten any possible sentence. My dad needed a get-out-of-jail-free card, only it wasn't free — he was paying for it, dearly. The legal costs were a constant insurmountable strain on my parents, as were the mental and emotional tolls. And in telling me, those costs were now also mine to bear.

"Perhaps you could write to tell the judge that I have suffered enough?" he said. "Would you consider doing that for me, kid?"

My parents were trusting me to carry that burden with them, to be in unity with them, on the same team, all fighting together for the survival of our family. Finally, it seemed as though they thought I was capable of knowing the truth and navigating it with them. I felt sad for my dad and the weight he'd been bearing, but I also felt relieved to be included, to belong.

I said yes.

When I finally mustered the courage to get on the phone with Worthbern and gather the detailed instructions that I needed to write the character reference, I was shocked by how much he knew about me. I sat on the edge of a twin bed in the corner of my dorm room and tried to steady my breath.

"How are you?" Worthbern said.

"Fine," I lied, brushing past his attempts at familiarity.

"How's the play going?" he asked. "Are you enjoying being an RA? Your folks told me those freshmen on your floor have been driving you crazy...."

Worthbern had spent more than a decade in a relationship with my parents that included intimate disclosures about people, places, and situations that defined their lives. I had not been given that same access and intimacy. Up until that week I hadn't known that he'd even existed—he didn't have the right to know so much about us. But this lawyer knew it all. About my family, about our secrets, and about me. His ease was proportional to the amount of time he'd spent gathering information about my life.

With that call to Worthbern, I was horrified to realize how much of an invisible fixture he had been in my life. And I finally understood that I became invisible that day in the elevator years earlier not because of anything I had done wrong, but because of my parents' inability to address the painful realities that they were trying to ignore, and their desire to protect me from those same painful realities.

~✼~

"How are you?" Worthbern had asked.

I hated that question. I couldn't have answered it, not fully. Swimming inside me was an ocean of complex emotions, ranging from fear and embarrassment to courage and hope. But I barely knew this man, and I had only just learned about the situation we were now discussing. "Fine," it seemed, was the only appropriate response.

But I wasn't fine. Something in his familiarity with me, and the ease with which he thought we could be in relationship with each other—the casual way that he asked me about the details of my life that he should not have been privy to—made me furious.

Often when I hear "How are you?" I am overcome with blind rage. My throat gets tight, my heart races, I feel hot behind my eyes, and my jaw clenches with the hopes of muzzling a response that will require an apology once this fit of anger passes.

I don't know how I am and even if I did, I don't know if I'd want to tell you.

How are you? Who are you? What do you want? How do you feel? I have struggled with these questions for a long time because these questions have been unimaginably difficult for me to answer.

For a lot of people, these are just everyday questions. For me, however, they have been terrifying threats to my reality. It is not the questions themselves—I love to present them to other people. I also feel blessed to have made a career out of asking these questions of imaginary characters. With every new role, I make bold decisions about who a character is and how they feel and what they want. But for as long as I can remember, whenever people ask me these very same questions, my response is often to panic. You wouldn't know that I am panicking. I am far too adept at the performance of control to let you perceive that there is an issue. What you see when you ask me one of those questions probably looks like a thoughtful reflection or a measured pause, but more often than not, inside, I am undone.

How am I? How the fuck should I know?

CHAPTER SEVEN

AN EDUCATION

There was never a question in my parents' mind about whether I was going to college.

With the unintended pressure to book work that had been placed on me by my parents, I had grown confused and ambivalent about what my relationship to acting had become. The work that felt most fulfilling now was the kind connected to arts education and activism—the work that I was doing with S.T.A.R. theater. I was still auditioning for film and television roles, but the question of college lay on the horizon.

My mother had been the first child in her family to obtain a college degree. She had gone on to receive a master's and a doctorate and was now a professor of education. My dad had a degree in business; my Aunt Daph was an assistant principal at a New York City high school. Most of my older cousins had gone to college. My grandma Isabelle's first and second grandchildren had both gone to medical school. My parents had sacrificed endlessly to afford an elite secondary education that would help pave the way for my future in academics and then in life.

But Katherine Atkinson, and a few other agents at J. Michael Bloom, had said that my star was rising. Kathy, who I've been working with for thirty years now, believed in me from the start. Casting directors were beginning to know my name, producers were responding to my work—"Now," they insisted, "was not the time to leave." A huge opportunity presented itself when I was asked to read for the role of Sally Hemings in a Merchant Ivory film, *Jefferson in Paris*. I was called back to read for producers several times and finally learned that the decision had come down to either me or the same British actor whom Juliet Taylor had cast in *Interview with the Vampire*, Thandiwe Newton. I told my team that if I got the Sally Hemings role, I would defer college and continue to pursue a career in acting.

But the part went to the exquisite Thandiwe, and I went to the George Washington University in Washington, DC.

~⁓~

I had chosen to go to GWU—a much larger school than many of the schools my Spence classmates had picked—because they offered the most financial aid, and because I was looking for a sense of belonging. To find that belonging, I needed room to explore and discover who I was. I needed to cast a wide net and make sure that the people I'd be meeting would expand my world, and that the opportunities to discover myself would be wide-ranging.

In addition to the great financial aid package, GWU offered me an academic scholarship as well as one of their Presidential art scholarships, for acting. I was even granted work-study in the costume and scene shops of the theater department. Although I hadn't broken through to enormous success on-screen, this hobby that I loved was actually providing serious financial benefits and also something else — independence.

GWU was my first time living away from Pugsley Avenue. DC was only a five-hour drive from New York City, but I was no longer in the cocooned care of my loving parents and a tony Upper East Side prep school. For all that I had learned as both a student and a peer educator, there was a lot I didn't know. I barely knew how to feed myself, didn't know how to balance a checkbook, had never done my own laundry. So, one afternoon, when the head of the costume department told me to press a dress, I literally went to a table and started to press down on the garment. He laughed, assuming it was a joke. And then he shook his head in disbelief when he realized that I was not trying to be funny. My mother eventually explained that she was attempting to free me from chores to make time for me to pursue my passions. But shielding me from learning the logistics of self-care meant that I had been groomed for success, but not self-sufficiency. For some reason she didn't feel she could give me both.

～～～

Before I left for GWU, auditioning in New York City had become difficult not only because of the pressure to book and the need to earn, but also because of the multiple tensions of not feeling attractive enough to win roles, attempting to conform to casting directors' ideas of what was attractive, and then finding myself catcalled and hassled out on the streets because I was traveling to and from auditions dressed in the ways I thought I had to.

But at GWU, the need to be desirable got divorced from the opportunities to act. So rather than objectifying myself, I could focus on acting and the business attached to it. It was in college that I fell more deeply in love with "the craft." With my scholarship I was being paid not just to act, but to *learn* how to act; I was given a toolbox to access and harness the magic. The focus was on process rather than booking jobs. I didn't have to walk in the room thinking about my appearance unless it was relevant to the character and the story. I learned to be in service to the material itself.

Due to the requirements of my scholarship, I had to audition for every single production, even for shows I was unable to be cast in due to the scheduling of other productions I was already committed to.

Auditioning can be brutal. As an actor, there is no piano to sit at, no instrument to hide behind. You are the instrument of your expression, and your humanity is on the line. Decisions will be made about whether to reward you not based on whether you can kick your leg high enough or sing the notes low enough—what is evaluated instead is... you. Sometimes there is small talk, and in this brief window you try to simultaneously project warmth and likeability while also keeping your brain focused on the specificity and intensity required of the scene work that you will soon have to drop into. You stand in front of a group of decision makers—mostly strangers, at least at the beginning of your career—and you let them ogle you, evaluate you, and judge you before you utter a word. Because of this, you must painstakingly think through every choice—how to dress and wear your hair and what makeup to apply—because when you enter that casting office, your body is a walking billboard for whether or not you are "the one."

Auditioning is one of the areas in my life where I learned the hard way that I needed to take hold of the concept of success and wrangle it away from the grip of others to define it for myself. This may sound strange coming from a person who is considered generally successful, but I don't do well when my goal is to be liked, loved, popular, or famous. I can't control what other people think of me, and when I try, even now, I can lose a sense of myself and get pulled back into feelings of fear and weakness, and into that ominous feeling I had growing up that something was wrong, and that the only way to fix it is to be as perfect as possible. Only, as an actor, it's not just the love of my parents that I am gunning for; it's the adoration of millions of fans, viewers, followers, and critics.

At GWU, I started to develop an entirely different orientation toward preparing for auditions. Auditions became my time in the lab to explore the ideas and frameworks I was being taught in class. I was being taught to analyze and break down dramatic literature, to approach a play through an academic lens. This was my first exposure to pure scene study without the promise of an audience or the end goal of securing a job. Reading for a role no longer became a test of my value, my ability to win, my beauty, my perfection, or even my talent. I started to see auditions as simply a gift and an opportunity. They became moments in time when I had full permission to use my imagination—to play, create, discover, and just have fun. They were invitations to spend fifteen minutes of the day doing what I loved to do, and then letting go of the results.

~~~

Although my parents dreamed of a much more traditional career path for me, by the time I made it halfway through college, I knew that I wanted to at least attempt to pursue a professional career in acting. Up to that point, becoming an actor had never seemed like a reasonable occupational goal. Despite my years of auditioning and working professionally both onstage and on the small screen (as TV was referred to back then), I held in my mind the notion that to want to be an actor meant that you had to want to be famous. And I had neither the hunger for fame nor the belief that I could achieve it.

I spent the summer between my sophomore and junior years studying just around the corner from TADA! in New York City at the Michael Howard Studios, and as part of our summer conservatory education, we had each been required to take a class called "Acting as a Business." In scene study class we studied our characters' objectives, obstacles, and given circumstances. In movement class, we learned about our centers of gravity, unconscious movement patterns, and breath work. But in "Acting as a Business," we learned to view ourselves as active participants in the goals we wanted to achieve.

The class was taught by veteran actor Caryn West and was meant to offer each of us a straight-talk approach to thinking about ourselves not just as artists, but as the entrepreneurs, salespeople, and marketing executives — basically, the CEOs — of our own creative lives. We learned that too often actors are taught to focus on the art of their performance without being taught how to think proactively and strategically as professionals in the workplace. We talked about how to pursue work, how to obtain representation, the best ways to supplement our income on the way to our dreams, and the day-to-day resources available to us as we worked to craft a life in the arts.

It was in that class that I first began to understand that as an actor you are both the producer and the product, the marketer and marketed, the driver of innovation and the passenger on the unpredictable ride that is show business. And it was also in that class that I first became aware of actors' unions. I had joined the Screen Actors Guild years before as a result of getting a speaking role in an ABC after-school special entitled *My Special Angel* (in which I played an unnamed high school cheerleader), but I was too young at the time to understand its value and significance.

When the subject emerged in "Acting as a Business" class, I was older and had studied the important role that unions have played in protecting the rights of workers in our country. As I sat in that class, I realized that if there were multiple unions for actors — Equity, SAG, and AFTRA (the latter two had not yet joined forces) — that meant that there must be an entire community of working actors making a decent living wage. It is frighteningly true that at any given moment over 90 percent of members in SAG are unemployed, and the odds of becoming a working actor are much slimmer than the odds of being successful in many non–show business fields. But the existence of several flourishing actors' unions signaled to me that wanting to be an actor did not necessarily mean that you had to want to be a famous movie star. "Making it" as an actor did not have to equate to perfection or fame or superstardom or being universally adored.

I desperately wanted to work as an actor, but I felt unworthy of success as a star because I felt more comfortable hiding behind my characters. I wanted people to love the characters, but never felt able to make them love me. Famous people, I thought, were famous for being themselves, but that didn't feel like it was meant for me. I didn't believe I was star quality. I just wanted to work, to make a living becoming other people, and I wanted those people, those characters, to have an impact on the lives of their audiences.

As I sat in that class and learned about the landscape of working artists and artisans who made up our guilds, I decided to attempt to be just that: a worker among workers. And in many ways that remains the goal.

It's the work that excites me more than anything. I appreciate the results, I enjoy the premieres, I'm grateful for the magazine covers…but it's the hard dig that I love, the rehearsals and the discovery process and the scene setting and the fight prep and finding the perfect shoe. What's happening in this scene? What do these characters want? What are the emotional stakes? What's the historical context? What is the story being told and why does it matter? The dramaturgy: that's what I love, and that's what I learned at GWU.

My cousin Rahim calls me "the longshoreman of acting," which has a special resonance for me because our grandfather was a longshoreman on the docks of Lower Manhattan. He died in 1953 in the middle of a nor'easter.

I like to think that I'd go into any storm to get the work done, too.

~~

After my summer at Michael Howard Studios, I was determined to pursue a professional life in the arts, but I wanted to use the last two years of college to understand everything about the history of performance and how it operates in the world, as well as the role that performance plays in our everyday lives—how we perform our thoughts, feelings, and identities. I designed an interdisciplinary major for myself titled "Performance Studies," in which I explored performance in various societies and cultures through both a social science and a fine arts lens.

For my thesis show, I defined myself in various ways—as a woman, Black person, daughter, activist—and developed a one-woman piece with a vignette for each aspect of my identity using music, dance, monologue work, and anthropological role play. I performed the show in a black-box theater with the support of fellow students serving in various crew positions in stage management and choreography.

I was trying to figure myself out. Performance had become not only my greatest passion but also my way of navigating through life, being who I thought I had to be or who others wanted me to be. It had become so integral to my existence that studying it was my attempt at taking the mask off performance itself, hoping to find myself.

To perform meant to deliver excellence and to meet, if not exceed, expectations. More than anything, acting for me was the magical practice of using detailed characters and specific stories to be a mirror, to reflect some truths about humanity back to an audience that does not see us, the actors, but rather sees a version of themselves. To perform also meant to devote myself to a creative process of expression that allowed me to transform and often disappear. So those two versions of me became even more pronounced: "Kerry," who was rooted, always, in the search for perfectionism and approval; and the more real me, who felt most comfortable when afforded the invisibility that resulted from pouring myself into an imaginary character. I embraced both performances in order to survive. To exist was to perform. And so, I was never not onstage.

But none of the roles I played in my everyday life were rooted in my truest self. The pathway to knowing my truth clearly had been broken before the bones in me were fully set. So, I searched for that version of me, and wondered who she was.

~~~

In my junior year of college, life had become unmanageable. I was still working as an RA in GWU's infamous Thurston Hall, a hall filled entirely with hormonal co-ed students living away from home for the very first time, kids constantly testing the boundaries of their bodies' capacity to metabolize drugs and alcohol. My job as an RA was to inspire them, monitor them, guide them, and to be both a role model and an enforcer of the university's policies and rules. To get the job, and the benefits that came with it (free room and board and a monthly stipend), I had fooled everyone into thinking that I was a highly respon sible, dependable, even-tempered, trustworthy, and upstanding member of the George Washington University community.

The truth was more complicated. Behind closed doors, I was an emotional wreck. Part of my internal upheaval was due to what was happening with my dad.

As the terrifying specter of a court date approached, I wrote the letter for Worthbern, both defending my dad's character and arguing for leniency in his sentencing. When it finally arrived, I requested time off from my RA duties, skipped class, and made the trip north to New York.

It was my first time in a court of law; it was also my first time meeting Worthbern in person. When we walked in the anteroom, he introduced himself, but there was no small talk this time—he was focused on my dad and reviewing all the protocols and possible outcomes.

My mother sat quietly; she seemed petrified. Her eyes remained locked on the table in front of us, but there was nothing there to stare at—just the table itself. I wondered what was going on behind her eyes, if she was questioning how she wound up in this position, or if she was imagining the shape that her life would take when faced with an incarcerated husband.

Unsure of what to do or say in the moments before we entered the courtroom for the sentencing, I stood behind my dad, running my hands along his shoulders, attempting to reduce his tension and fear, unwilling and unable to process my own. The only reference point I had for what I saw in my dad's body language was the posture of the kids that I had stumbled upon engaged in illicit behavior at Thurston. As RAs we were required to hang signs around the floor that detailed when we'd be doing room inspections. In our first meetings with our students, we would implore them: "We don't want to catch you— the last thing we want to do is file an incident report at one o'clock on a Saturday morning. So, we are giving you fair warning. You know when we're coming. Please don't get caught." But inevitably, there were those students who wound up sitting in a room answering questions, detailing their sins for me to report to the university and for the university to report to their parents. It was the anticipation of the punishment that laid ahead, the dread of facing consequences, that directed their gaze downward, curved their shoulders forward, and filled every limb with lead.

That was how my dad looked that day.

When the judge arrived, I searched his face for clues to our family's future. But his expression gave nothing away. In the end, the hearing was surprisingly quick, and rather than receive any time in prison, my dad was required to pay penalties to the IRS and perform community service. What followed was immense relief and joy; my parents were finally able to let go of a decade-long investigation and legal struggle. They had come to the end of a nightmare journey. I knew we would never talk about it again. Being included in this secret trauma did not mean general transparency. Still, I was grateful for the leniency of my dad's sentencing and moved to witness the release of demons that had chased them for far too long.

But something in me was still at sea.

~~~

If my dream was to be a worker among workers, I had to find work.

My life as an actor after college would include countless rejections; soul-crushing auditions for everything from fast-food commercials to educational training videos; small roles in large productions where I was asked to do things I simply wasn't comfortable doing; and, like so many fledgling actors, a side hustle that paid the bills.

With a sense and maybe even a fear of what lay ahead, I wanted to ground myself in an experience that could remind me of the precious nature of pure performance outside of the framework of the business. I resolved to spend some time overseas after graduation, before moving back to New York and into my parents' apartment. This would accomplish two things: One, I would have the opportunity to live in a country and study a performance tradition that was rooted in history, culture, identity, and spirituality; and two, I would give myself a chance to explore the world before going back to live in the same bedroom that I had slept in as that frightened little girl.

～ᴄᴏ～

I chose India for a few reasons. I wanted to study performance in a place where theater was sacred. I wanted to be able to step onstage and participate in a theater tradition filled with history and divinity so that perhaps I could endure the hustle that was to come and focus on the thing that I loved most about acting—the embodiment of story performed in service of the human experience. Knowing that I would be faced with a business that would seek to objectify, marginalize, and "otherize" me, I wanted first to embrace, and thereafter always remember, the sacred shared humanity at the root of great acting, and great artwork of any kind. Travel, I hoped, would enhance my ability to understand and create characters by enriching my knowledge and experience of how different people live all around the world.

The other reason I wanted to go to India was to get closer to God.

～ᴄᴏ～

For as long as I can remember, food had been my comfort.

As a latchkey kid with two working parents, I used to awake in the mornings to the sounds and smells of my mother cooking that day's dinner. She would leave it in the refrigerator, encased in Saran wrap, with a Post-it note detailing any additional reheating instructions. Each note was signed, "Love ya," which once caused my cousin Jared to ask, "Who's 'ya'?" Food from my mother was my comfort—it was how she loved me from afar. And when I ate, I felt less lonely, even if only for a moment.

But food as emotional comfort can be problematic. When food is detached from physical nourishment and used predominantly as a tool to either feel better or feel nothing, there comes a time when there is not enough food in the world to fill the void.

By the time I got to college, my relationship with food and my body had become a toxic cycle of self-abuse that utilized the tools of starvation, binge eating, body obsession, and compulsive exercise. I would, when seeking to stuff my feelings, stuff my face, secretly binge eating for days at a time, often to the point of physical pain, sometimes to the point of passing out. Then, awake the next morning surrounded by dirty dishes, empty food boxes, and sticky leftovers, I would resolve to rid my body of the comfort I had sought the night before. But not by throwing up; that was too messy—that behavior was for girls with eating disorders, girls who were weak and undisciplined. Instead, my drive toward perfectionism directed me toward control, either by not eating for days at a time, or by exercising for several hours, all in an attempt to right the wrongs of the bingeing.

And though they eventually led to unfathomable levels of depression, food and exercise were at first ideal ways to indulge compulsive behaviors because I could hide them more easily than drugs or alcohol. And that constant manipulation of my own behavior allowed me the illusion of control.

This excessive swinging between extremes was accompanied by a consistent hatred of my body. If my childhood had been spent in the constant pursuit of being better, the seeds of perfectionism had blossomed into self-contempt.

When I tried to talk about it with friends and family, I was told that "Everyone eats when they're upset," and that "Exercise is good for you." Maybe people were unable to see me as being sick, messy, and flawed, or they reacted that way because of how our culture has normalized the insanity around food and body image.

But I had lost control, and I knew it. My entire life revolved around the vicious cycle of hating what I saw in the mirror, using food to comfort and quiet those thoughts and feelings, and then punishing myself with exercise and starvation to try to fix this body that seemed to be the source of all my pain. I was at war with myself. There seemed to be no escape from the demons; that hopelessness and agony led to thoughts of suicide. And I started to realize that I couldn't fix this on my own.

Late at night, all alone, away from home and hiding from all those freshmen, I found myself on my knees, begging for guidance. Although I had grown up in a family that occasionally attended church on holidays or for special occasions, this was the first time I'd ever made a direct request. *Please, God, help me.*

In the weeks that followed, I started therapy, both one-on-one and in group settings. The performance I'd been maintaining for close to two decades began to ebb away. I began learning to embrace my truth, to have my feelings, to allow myself to be messy and imperfect and human. I learned that I was not alone in my suffering. And a newfound relationship with the Divine began to guide me toward more loving-kindness for myself, more gratitude for my life, and more awareness of the sacred power of everything around me.

CHAPTER EIGHT

MONSOON SEASON

It doesn't get any messier and more sacred and human and potent than India. And that's why at the end of college I applied for a program in South India to study Kathakali, the captivating theatrical tradition of India where actors paint their faces in enormous, often green, mask-like countenances and move across the stage in highly stylized movements with almost operatic emotions. I would have the opportunity to study this form of acting, but the program's advisors suggested that if I wanted to understand movement arts in India, and become deeply connected to the way the culture lives in the body, then I should spend my time devoted to two ancient South Indian movement arts: Kalarypayattu, a martial art that is thought to sit at the root of all the other performance traditions of South India, and yoga.

~~~

My first exposure to yoga had occurred in a stuffy drawing room on the sixth floor of the Spence School. My PE teacher, Ms. Checken, would use the space to introduce our class to the practice.

Although I didn't consider myself an athlete, I liked Ms. Checken a lot, so when she told me I might like yoga, I stood on the mat that first day with an open mind. I barely remember the physical positions we were taught in the first half of the class—but I do remember how I felt. It was a new feeling, a feeling of being fully present and alive. I felt like I was inside my skin, as though my cells themselves were breathing. It was as if my fullest sense of self was embodied within the walls of my physical being. And until that moment, I did not know that this was a way to be in the world. Up until then, the closest feeling I'd had was the feeling of aliveness I experienced when I was in water, or when I was onstage pretending to be somebody else. But this was a sense of full presence, on land, as me.

I remember Ms. Checken telling us to find our balance by choosing a point on the wall of the drawing room and centering our focus there. But I had nowhere to look—those walls were covered in appalling depictions of early colonial life in the United States, including Indigenous Americans and enslaved Africans. There was nowhere for me to focus without being confronted by a wallpapered presentation of my ancestry, meant to reinforce false notions about my racial inferiority. Instead, I chose to close my eyes and look within.

What I remember most viscerally about my first yoga class, however, was the end of it. Ms. Checken described the final position of the class as "corpse pose"—Shavasana. This asana, she explained, is usually the final position in any yoga practice. Its purpose is to fully rest the body in a deep state of relaxation and meditation before moving on with the day. As we lay on our backs as directed—with our palms facing up and our feet hip-width apart—Ms. Checken walked us through a guided meditation. She asked us to tense and tighten individual body parts for a count of three and then release and relax each one— first our hands, then our forearms, then our ears, noses, all the way down to our toes. She told us to imagine with each breath that every single part of our body was sinking deeper into the floor beneath us.

And then she stopped talking.

And we just lay there, breathing.

I started to weep. I had spent thirty minutes flowing through poses that moved me into a deep physical connection with myself. I was fully awake in my body, lying on that mat, with nowhere to go—no distractions, no performance, no urge for perfectionism. Just me.

I had no memory of ever feeling this way before. I felt safe, and I had spent most of my life *not* feeling safe. I understood the tears that were melting out of me only as confusion and disorientation at the time, but those tears were also an outpouring of grief for the hypervigilant little girl who lived within me. She had learned long ago that rest and relaxation were hazardous states of being. She had not slept for years, trying to protect herself, terrified of the things that transpired in the night. And even in the daytime, she had avoided being fully awake in her body to skirt the memories of those same terrors, and to escape the disconnect all around her and the loneliness it produced.

As Ms. Checken invited us to wiggle our toes and begin to come out of our meditation, I wiped my tears and tried to steady my breath. I was shocked by the power I had drawn from mindful movement, and then by the feelings the simplicity of silence and stillness had evoked in me. Safety had led to grief. And yoga had led to some kind of deep physical and emotional thawing that felt more like the real me.

Yoga would become a bridge back to wholeness, physically, emotionally, and spiritually. I started to find space within my body, to rest and reside within it. And I started to understand that there was strength to be found in stillness and determination required on the journey toward flexibility. One translation of the Sanskrit word "yoga" is "to yoke"—yoking myself to yoga became a new way to think about everything, including my relationship with myself. Even in college and after, in the midst of a binge, I would turn to yoga to confront my demons, accept the insanity, love myself, stop the behavior, and reset.

Yoga, I learned, was not just a form of exercise, but a way of life.

~~~

My time in India would be drenched in God. There was no escaping it, which was good because I had no desire to do so. Two years of treatment for my depression and eating disorder had led me on an emotional and spiritual journey. In looking to heal my relationship with food and my body, I was learning to seek peace in the comfort of a higher power, rather than in the endorphin spike of compulsive bingeing, or the numbing results of abusive starvation, or even the false belief that all would be well if I could attain whatever body I had come to believe was perfect. I was beginning to embrace the idea that surrendering to a power greater than myself, a power I was starting to refer to as "God," was a more reliable pathway to peace than the pursuit of perfection.

Everywhere I turned in India, God—and the many forms in which God manifests in the Hindu tradition—was present. From the phrase most used to greet others—"namaste," which translates to "the God in me salutes the God in you"—to the altars in every home, business, and even on the sides of the road, God was in all things. God was in people, and places, and situations that took me out of my comfort zone—the language, the food, the culture, and most especially for me, in the deep traditions of centuries-old movement and performing arts.

I felt fully alive in India. It made sense to me that yoga would be born in this place, a place that so strongly invites the awakening of the senses. As in my yoga practice, I knew that I'd have to stretch beyond the comforts of the familiar to keep up with its teeming magic.

～～

There were five students and an academic advisor/chaperone/translator, Don, in the program. We were based in the capital of Kerala: Thiruvananthapuram, a city Mahatma Gandhi once referred to as "the evergreen city of India." (Thiruvananthapu-ram had once been called Trivandrum but had more recently reclaimed its Indian heritage and was using its original name.)

While, at the time, the mid-southern regions of India were modernizing and embracing technology and Western customs and dress, Kerala was still very much in thrall to tradition. From the time we arrived in Kerala until the end of my studies, when I traveled farther north to Bangalore (now Bengalaru), I never saw a woman dressed in Western attire (aside from one white tourist while changing buses in the center of town). Most of the clothes that I brought with me to India would remain unused. Upon arrival we were taken to a shop to replace our Western jeans and T-shirts with saris for special occasions, and for everyday attire, elegantly embroidered salwar kameez, a traditional ensemble worn by both women and men that consists of loose-fitting pajama-like trousers and a long shirt or tunic top.

It was clear even from our first few days that Kerala was a region bursting with ritual, tradition, art, culture, and history.

Our two-story house was on a quiet street in an idyllic residential section of the city. The students' bedrooms were on the top floor. Don stayed in a room downstairs, and Tangama, our house mother—a local woman who served as chef and housekeeper, as well as our eyes and ears, and connection to the neighborhood—lived in a room at the back of the house. Don spoke fluent Malayalam and had captured not just the vocabulary and the grammar but the tonality of the speech and its accompanying body language. He spent years integrating himself into the community by living and studying in Kerala, building relationships, and now bringing students there. At GWU I'd learned to approach theater with the mind of an anthropologist. I marveled at Don's ability to belong without performing—he didn't pretend to be one of the locals. He respectfully devoted himself to the rhythm and the song and the physicality of South Indian culture, but he remained Don, authentically true to himself. I wondered if India could help me find a similar authenticity.

Five days a week, just before dawn, I was awoken by the prayer calls emitted from the speakers on the roof of the temple that stood across our small street. Metallic in tone, those melodic cries pierced through the morning twilight and beckoned my eyes open.

Because of its tropical climate and terrain, the cornerstone of South Indian cuisine is coconut, and every evening Tangama prepared for the following day either idili (a small, soft, fluffy cake made from steamed fermented rice and lentil batter), appam (soft, thin, flat hoppers made from fermented rice and coconut batter), or parotta (a flaky flatbread reminiscent of croissant), served with a sambar and a rich coconut chutney on the side. In the morning, alone at the dining table, I would light a candle or small lantern and savor the fragrant meal while reading from one of a few daily meditations that I had brought with me from the States.

Once my meal was finished, with the rest of the house still asleep, I would walk to the door, where all of our shoes were kept (shoes were not worn inside the home), slide my shoes on, bow to the altar that sat next to our television, and venture out into the warm monsoon air to walk the two miles into town to the studio, where I would begin my Kalarypayattu lessons.

With the sun slowly peeking through the palm trees, I passed tailor shops, grocery stores, temples, and beauty salons, all covered in the sensual curvatures of the Malayalam alphabet.

For my Kalarypayattu training, I had purchased loose-fitting fight pants—the standard uniform for learning this dance-like battle—and donned one of my T-shirts from home. As I got closer to class, the town awakened with me, and my arrival—strange at first, this African American woman with braids in her hair, Western T-shirts, and traditional Indian pants—began to fold itself into the morning rituals of the neighborhood.

What began as a mysterious walk in an unknown land became a sacred routine of smiles and namastes, where, with time, I went from being delightfully overwhelmed by all new sights, sounds, and smells, to becoming more attuned to the subtle differences and shifts in the life of the community. I noticed when the altars were refreshed and when the tailors received new shipments of fabrics from the north. I knew to listen for the cries of a baby waking up like clockwork every morning as I passed her window, and I smiled when I noticed the fat brown alley cat had birthed her new litter.

When I arrived at the studio, called the Kalari, I was led through a seemingly endless series of calisthenic-type warm-up kicks and stretches before fight training began. We were a small group—just me with my teacher, his apprentice, and occasionally one other female student, Daphne, who was visiting Kerala from Paris.

The warm-ups began with a series of salutations, akin to yoga's sun salutations. In this case, however, they were performed in reverence to the presiding deities of the Kalari—the building, the practice, and the traditions of the fight.

It is important to clarify that, at the time, I didn't consider myself a fighter. I came to India to study the arts and meditation. I spent an entire childhood in the Bronx and was never in a single fistfight. That's not to say that I didn't see fights in my neighborhood—in the back of the schoolyard, or on the platform of the number 6 train, or at the corner outside the pizza shop. I witnessed both childish scraps and raw brutality more than once, but I somehow slid through my time in the Bronx without ever having to throw down, maybe partly because I was the cousin of John, Rahim, and Jared, and people knew that they would protect me.

But now here I was, on the other side of the globe, learning to fight like the ancient warriors of southeast Asia. According to legend, the Hindu god Parashurama learned Kalarypayattu—the art of the battlefield—from the Lord Shiva and taught the fight to the original settlers of Kerala soon after he brought Kerala up to the surface from the bottom of the sea. I was taught that Kathakali performers who studied both yoga and Kalarypayattu were believed to be much more talented and proficient than their counterparts, and that if I wanted to understand and study the great tradition of Indian theater, then my afternoons were best spent devoting myself to yoga, and my mornings were best spent learning to fight.

Traditionally, the floor of every Kalari is made from thick red sand blended with ayurvedic herbs that are believed to help heal the wounds garnered during fight training. Because it was monsoon season, the air was thick, and at the end of each morning's battle practice, I left drenched in sweat and mud and dust...and joy. On my walk home I tracked the fragrant smell of that healing clay through my neighborhood, now wholly awake and bustling with life. And if I was lucky, at some point on my walk home, the sky would open with the violent torrents of a passing storm, cleansing my path and me and refreshing my spirit from the arduous morning workout.

Before lunch, three days a week, the five of us worked with Don on our Malayalam. We were not only learning phrases and vocabulary that would be useful in our everyday exchanges and help us to build relationships within our community, but also learning to read and write the ancient alphabet itself. I am forever grateful for the experience of walking to training in the morning and attempting to sound out syllables of Malayalam that appeared on the stores' signs. I had no expectation of understanding the words I was reading, but I hoped I would remember which shapes elicited which sounds.

India is a continent with many regional languages, and while the national language is Hindi, the second most common language spoken across India is English. A reward came for me one morning when, as I was sounding out the letters, my mouth formed the sounds, "Bee-Ay-Ooo-Tee-Sh-Op." I gasped and looked down into the windows below the sign and saw the hoods of two hair dryers and three swivel seats in front of large mirrors. I felt triumphant, and proud, and grateful to have the opportunity to be stretching my mind and humbling myself as a traveler in the unknown.

~~~

It is strange how memory works. In my life, there are things that I remember with clarity and other things that remain a disjointed blur. Many of my early memories are disturbingly faint. I wonder if this is the result of being told that my truth was not my own. *Why remember the details if they aren't even real? Why store narrative in a brain that can't be trusted?* I know that this is also a common result of trauma, and of sexual trauma in particular. And yet those memories of sexual violation are some of the clearest memories I have.

One morning, on the way to the Kalari, as I turned left at the corner of our deserted, nest-like street, in the distance I saw a boy on a bike riding toward me. I passed him regularly, though I rarely saw anyone else on this part of the walk. This long road eventually led to a second corner with a tiny store that sold odd knickknacks and snacks, smoking supplies, phone cards, and time for using one of the two public landlines.

As the boy on the bike got closer, I could see that he was as usual delivering newspapers. There were a few elegantly spread out homes on this road, and he was tossing the *Malayala Manorama* toward their entryways. As he passed me, I could sense his fascination with me. My skin tone was closer to the hues of South Indians than any of my housemates. In the southern regions of India, the melanin in skin tones has adapted for protection in the same way that it has in the continent of Africa, where my ancestors are from. It was not uncommon for me to encounter South Indians with skin darker than mine, and I felt a kinship with darker-skinned Indians.

I was often asked if my family was from Kerala, or if either parent perhaps was of Indian descent. I usually laughed because this was a question that I got in other parts of the world, too. Throughout my life I have been questioned about where my family might be from. I felt that these questions intimated a desire for me to belong within their tribe — Nigerian, Ethiopian, Dominican, Cuban, Indian. As a student of culture and identity — and as someone longing for a deeper sense of self — I was delighted by the invitation to belong to people all over the world.

For many years I understood the question as legitimate. My grandfather had jokingly speculated about the true ethnic identity of my mother and her sisters. But as I got older, I also understood the racism that was embedded in this questioning. Colorism had built a gradient scale of human value based on the relative degree of Blackness in a person. To mix one's Blackness with "other" became a way to rise out of the perceived curse of Blackness.

I thought the boy on the bike was curious about me in the ways my grandfather had been curious about my mother — who is she, where is she from?

I pondered all this as he approached, expecting him to pass me by and continue to deliver his papers. But as he reached me, he thrust out his hand and aggressively grabbed my left breast. I screamed and jumped back, looking up and down this peaceful road. But dawn was breaking and there was no one else there. The boy kept pedaling away while looking back at me, somehow shocked that I hadn't liked his violent advance. I kept my eye on him, walking backward toward the Kalari, until he was out of sight.

I couldn't focus on training that morning; my movements were disjointed, my coordination sloppy. And even my walk home was different. Though the sun was up, and the streets were full of people, on that day I was afraid.

I knew that I would see the boy the next morning, so I told Don what had happened and watched my fear become his rage. Because he was a trusted member of the community, Don was able to do some neighborhood detective work, identify the kid, reach out to his parents, reprimand him with their permission, and get a promise that it would never happen again.

Don explained to me that as he was scolding the young man, the boy kept referencing *Baywatch*. As we discussed it, we realized that the images of Western women that are projected onto young men's minds all over the world are often hypersexualized. These portrayals falsely communicate the idea that the bodies of Western women are there for the taking. It was a powerful lesson in how representation in entertainment impacts culture and behavior everywhere.

～◯～

Eventually, it became clear that I would not be perform-ing Kathakali—Kalarypayattu and yoga would be all I was allowed to do. At first, I wondered why I was waking up at five in the morning to do calisthenics and fight training. Where were the elaborate costumes? Where was the green makeup? Where were the bright lights? What I learned was that it takes decades to be allowed onstage as a Kathakali actor. Although I came to India to study the theater, there was no way I would be allowed to participate in this tradition after just a few brief months. I watched the masters perform, but I didn't get to do so myself.

I thought that I went to India to be onstage. Instead, I real-ized I went there to be with myself. I let the movement arts of Kalarypayattu and yoga be my teachers. The stage was India itself; the story was my own. I had been baptized in the waters of the monsoon rains. I was receiving the daily gift of fable, ritual, culture, and wisdom.

When it was time to leave India, I felt I had done what I came to do—I had grounded myself in this ancient tradition. These art forms had put me more fully in my body and closer to my truth. Part of that truth was that I had more love, respect, and reverence for theater than ever before. Developing this deeper connection with myself, as well as an awareness that I was longing to get back onstage to participate firsthand in the magic, seeded within me the knowledge that I was ready.

To this day, Kathy Atkinson has a postcard hanging on the wall of her office. On the front is an image of traditional Keralan drummers engaged in ritual performance. On the back is a note from me, sent from the other side of the world, telling her that I was loving every moment of my adventure in India, but that I was also looking forward to returning to the States and pursuing a professional life in the arts.

CHAPTER NINE

MIRACLES

"Is this your real name?" Ellen Gilbert said, shaking her head. It was simply too perfect a pseudonym—easy to pronounce, easy to remember, unique but familiar, distinguished but friendly.

I was at Abrams Artists Agency for a meeting with Ellen, who was—and still is—a legendary talent agent for kids. Kathy Atkinson had left J. Michael Bloom to become a manager and had offered to represent me. When I returned from India, our first order of business was to find me representation with a new agency. At the time, I was fresh out of college, living with my parents, and although I was no longer a child, I was still able to get away with playing one. (Younger-looking twentysomethings are often hired to play adolescents because an actor can have the appearance of a minor without the need to curtail filming hours for child labor laws.)

This was not my first agency meeting since I'd gotten back from India. One agency hadn't been interested. The other had been willing to take me on, but only if I would make numerous changes to my appearance, including dental work and weight loss.

But this meeting with Ellen Gilbert felt different. Ellen is tiny—barely 5'1"—but her energy fills a room. That afternoon, I hung on her every word, feeling like my options for agent representation were dwindling and that if Abrams Artists did not take me on, maybe Kathy would lose faith in me, the way that I was already beginning to lose faith in myself.

But Ellen was all smiles.

"I loved your reading," she said, referring to the audition I had just performed. "I think you are adorable."

It had taken four years of college and a trip halfway around the world to finally feel ready to pursue a career as an actor. My heart swelled with gratitude, aglow with Ellen's approval.

"Yes," I said. "My name really is Kerry Washington." And then, with a shrug and a wide smile, I added, "I guess I was born with a stage name."

~~∽~~

I have had auditions in my career where I could tell that the opportunity was lost before the audition even began. Once, during a chemistry read (the term for a final callback where a lead actor will read scenes with a handful of potential costars so that the producers can decide who has the best chemistry), I could sense within about a minute or two that I was not the lead actor's first choice for the film, and that I had only been invited as a backup option. Another time I read with an esteemed actor who was directing his first feature. The word on the street was that the role was mine — people were calling Kathy and Ellen to congratulate us — but when I arrived at the final audition, I learned that there was, in fact, another actor in the mix, and that she had become the front-runner. And it felt as though the entire time the director was watching my audition, my choices were juxtaposed against his fantasy of how perfect that other actor would be in the role.

I didn't get either of these roles. Repeated rejection is a way of life for any actor. But each rejection weighed heavily on me. This was especially true at the beginning of my career, because when I heard no, it felt like a rejection of me personally. Every time I was not chosen to play a role, I slid back into those early feelings of invisibility, loneliness, and inadequacy.

The generally accepted purpose of an audition is to get a job. That's certainly what I thought in the beginning. Now, out of the creative cocoon of GWU, when I didn't get the job, time and again, I couldn't help but feel debilitated. If I poured my heart into preparing for an audition, gave my all in the room, was vulnerable and honest — and the role still went to someone else because of their height or their haircut, or because the sound of their voice reminded the director of the aunt who inspired him to write the film — well, none of that was in my control. I decided at some point that booking a job should not be the measure of success because it was not emotionally sustainable to keep doing my best, coming up empty-handed, and feeling like a failure.

So, I started to refocus my definition of success on process rather than on results. Had I tried my best? Had I given it my all? If I could honestly answer yes to both of those questions and it still did not go my way, then—out of necessity—I had to have faith in the belief that I was collecting these "nos" on the way to "yesses," and if the "yesses" never came, then I would know when it was time to move on.

I gave myself one year.

~~~

In the early years of an actor's career, most of your time is spent trying to obtain work—the job, therefore, is mostly to audition—and the reward is when you actually book a gig. The reality, however, is that more often than not, the role goes to someone else. At its root, auditioning is about solving someone's problem—writers, directors, and producers want to tell a story, but they need people to embody it and bring it to life. You can either be the exact right person for the role, or, if you're not, your audition might offer clarity about who it is they are looking for.

Eventually I would come to understand this view of auditioning, that it was a way to be of service. But at the time, I thought it was my job to try to be "the one." I had learned to see and trust God in so much of my life, but for some reason I had not embraced that faith in my acting career. In the real world, the repeated rejection that I received in audition rooms—and my desperate desire to avoid that rejection—

became a dangerous breeding ground for increased people-pleasing and perfectionism.

When I auditioned for the agency that had suggested I lose weight, it triggered demons that I'd been fighting to rein in.

The form of my food and exercise abuse had always been fluid. I was careful to avoid engaging in behavior that I thought fit a specific diagnosis. I thought I could avoid the stigma of having an eating disorder if I consistently switched up my compulsive behavior. But faced with the pressures of trying to make it in a business that relies so heavily on appearance, I slid back into the insanity of my behavior in college: binge eating, avoiding eating altogether, exercising for multiple hours a day, even adding laxatives and diuretics to the cycle of abuse.

Unlike in high school and college, weed and alcohol were no longer an option—I couldn't enjoy the feeling of being out of control. Using them didn't allow me to maintain the facade of perfection. Food and exercise were my drugs of choice because everyone eats and many people work out, so I could mask my abuse behind socially acceptable behavior and remain high-functioning in the midst of the maelstrom. But behind closed doors, the behavior was extreme. And the obsession was debilitating. I hated myself, which made me want to escape further into the emotional numbness that this abuse of my body provided.

~~~

When I auditioned for the role of Lanisha Brown in *Our Song*, I was twenty-two years old, but the character was fifteen. Lanisha was half Black, half Cuban. She had a distinct cultural fluency, and emotional sensitivity. She was thoughtful, studious, and curious — she reminded me of the girl I had been just a few years before. Although I had done some on-camera work in television and educational videos, *Our Song*, I hoped, would be my first film, and I wanted it so badly. Before auditioning, I watched Jim McKay's most recent film, *Girls Town*, a critically lauded movie that had won the Filmmakers' Trophy at Sundance. The vérité style of *Girls Town*, as well as Jim's insights into the realities of female adolescence, reminded me of the work we'd done at S.T.A.R. theater, only elevated into cinematic form.

I auditioned and got a callback, before which, at Jim's request, I did more physical preparation for the role by studying the posture of teenagers and remembering how they moved. After that second audition I got on my knees in the bathroom in Alexa Fogel's Tribeca casting office and prayed to get the role. "Please God," I begged, "I know I'm the right person for this."

Apparently, God agreed.

I'll never be as good again — never ever ever — as I was in that first movie.

Filmed entirely on location in Brooklyn during the summer of 1999, *Our Song* is the coming-of-age story of three best friends, Lanisha, Maria, and Joycelyn, who are members of a local marching band. Jim's commitment to portraying realism on-screen meant that we joined the real-life marching band that inspired the film, the Jackie Robinson Steppers. Although everyone knew we were making a film, to the other members of the band we were our characters; they had no idea how old we were and called us only by our characters' names. We three basically disappeared into the fabric of the community, while taking on its rhythms and mores. For these reasons, among others, Jim's movie is a deeply convincing portrayal of everyday life in Crown Heights and the young people who live there.

Jim lived in a walk-up apartment on Rivington Street on the Lower East Side of Manhattan. Before filming began, he hosted the three leads of the film—Melissa Martinez, Anna Simpson, and me—for rehearsals. Sitting around his kitchen table, we would discuss the characters' relationships, break down each scene, and examine every line. At one point Melissa, who played Maria, asked, "Hey, can we change the words sometimes? I mean, it's not like, Shakespeare, right?"

I looked at Jim, nervous that he might be upset. To many writers the comparison may have been offensive, but Jim was, in his heart, an anthropologist, a linguist—a social scientist. Like Don in South India, Jim had spent time in the community, listening to the rhythms of the way people spoke, hearing the poetry in their patois. From my perspective, what Jim had written on the page was Shakespeare in the same way that August Wilson is Shakespeare. Each is poetic discourse born out of culture and character specificity. But like all great directors, Jim is also a collaborator, and he knew that Melissa herself had an innate linguistic rhythm that was at times closer to her character than Jim's own imagination.

"Yeah, sure, we can play around with the language," he said, smiling. "Tell me what you want to say—let's figure it out together."

~~~

Our Song was shot on a budget of just $100,000. I loved the filming process—it was guerrilla filmmaking at its finest. Unable to afford permits, we "stole" several shots on the A train in Far Rockaway, at the edge of Queens, across the marshlands of Jamaica Bay from JFK Airport and not far from where my parents spent that first day at the beach. As we filmed, I looked out and saw a plane that had just taken off and realized that this was one of the first times in my life that I didn't want to be on it. That kid, standing in her living room, had always fantasized about being on those planes flying in and out of LaGuardia Airport. But now, I had found my escape. Not on a plane—I had escaped into this character, into this movie, and into the magic of filmmaking, a process that necessitates the embodiment of an alternate reality. Sitting on the A train as Lanisha Brown, I was exactly where I wanted to be.

~~~

On the morning that *Our Song* hit theaters, I was walking across Central Park to a group recovery meeting on the Upper West Side. I'd been back from India for a couple of years at this point and was doing the daily maintenance work to try to keep my obsessions with food and exercise and body image at bay. Some days were better than others.

These were the early days of cell phones, and service was spotty. When I finally reached Central Park West, I was at first concerned that something awful had happened because my phone was filled with voicemails and texts. But as I opened the messages, I found they were filled with excitement and congratulations. Unbeknownst to me, reviews of *Our Song* had just hit the press. As I listened, one voicemail in particular stood out—it was from Leslie Jacobson, the head of the theater department at George Washington University and one of my most beloved mentors. I could hear in her voice that she was trying to hold back tears.

"You *are* a miracle!" she said, but I didn't know what she meant. Later that morning I read A. O. Scott's *New York Times* review: "Watching Ms. Simpson, Ms. Martinez, and Ms. Washington, none of whom has appeared in a movie before, you forget that they are acting, which means they are acting very well indeed.... Ms. Washington is, simply, a miracle."

Our Song was a critical success and an indie film favorite. It premiered at Sundance, where it was nominated for the Grand Jury Prize, and went on to receive an Indie Spirit Award nomination for Best Feature. But I was unable to attend either Sundance or any awards shows because I was deep in production on my second film.

~~

I had to audition for *Save the Last Dance* multiple times. After several meetings with producers, it finally came down to another actor or me for the role of Chenille. The other actor was a high-profile pop star; I was an "unknown" who was still filming my first movie, a low-budget indie. The smart thing for the producers to do would have been to hire the pop star...but I wanted this role, and I fought for it.

Our Song had allowed me to use the toolbox I'd developed at S.T.A.R. I played a teenager dealing with issues of self-esteem, drug use, and teen sexuality. In fact, in one of the most intimidating scenes for me to film, I discussed my pregnancy and abortion with my mother. When I read *Save the Last Dance,* I knew that this was an opportunity to continue to do the same kind of work, bringing light to the real experience of a young woman of color, but this time on a larger stage.

Save the Last Dance was a huge studio movie, and my character, Chenille, was an unlikely hero at the time—for a start, she was a teen mom from inner-city Chicago. Chenille was charismatic and sparkly, a talented fashion designer, incredibly confident, and a bold shit-talker. She lived inside the aspirational part of me—she was a truth-teller who stood up to a deadbeat boyfriend like a superhero. And I knew her. She was the girls I grew up with.

So, in my final audition, when doing a scene scripted to take place in a playground, I made the choice to split my attention between my imaginary child swinging on an imaginary play structure and the other character in the scene. That creative impulse impressed our director, Thomas Carter, and seemed to cement the job as mine.

Kathy and Ellen received an official offer from Paramount Studios for me to play Chenille. But when it came time for the (always uncomfortable) negotiation process, my entire team tried to dissuade me from doing the movie. They felt I wasn't being offered enough money, and, in fact, my agent and manager were so pissed about the offer that they went out and got drunk and sent the bill to the casting director, Avy Kaufman.

In the end, though, the decision was mine, and my passion for the project prevailed.

And though this was my second film, the experience of making *Save the Last Dance* could not have been more different from making *Our Song*. On *Our Song* we changed into our costumes every day in the living room of an apartment in the government housing projects where we were filming. The costumes themselves were purchased from local discount department stores with secondhand items thrown in for added authenticity. On *Save the Last Dance,* I had elaborate costume fittings with designer clothes, and custom-tailored looks were laid out for me every morning in my trailer. On *Our Song,* there were no trailers—in fact, our transportation department consisted of the New York City MetroCards we were handed each week, and the occasional generosity of rides from my mother in her Subaru.

Then there was the food. On *Our Song,* we ate West Indian takeout and bought snacks from bodegas in Crown Heights.

On *Save the Last Dance,* we enjoyed lavish catering and craft services. At every meal break I would make a plate of food for myself and then a second plate to take home as leftovers because I was determined not to spend my per diem. I eventually saved enough cash from the per diem on *Save the Last Dance* (under my mattress at the hotel suite) that I was able to buy my first laptop computer.

But what remained consistent with my experience from *Our Song,* and what I'd learned in my acting training so far, was the importance of anthropological research. I tracked down a program in the Chicago school system for teen moms and spent time with the students there, absorbing details about how they organized their days and processed their feelings as student moms. I was also careful to bond with the infant twins who had been hired to play my child, visiting with them and their family (changing their diapers, feeding them, playing with them) so that we would be comfortable with each other in our scenes together.

But there was more required to understand the heart of Chenille. In addition to being a mother, she was a vibrant teenager who, along with the other characters in the film, indulged in Chicago nightlife. So as actors hired to tell this story, we had no choice but to do the same. Our choreographer, the legendary Fatima Robinson, would take us out dancing every night. Because we were known around town as actors in a movie, and because one of the members of Onyx, a then-famous hip-hop group, was in our cast, and because Fatima and her dancers had relationships with promoters all over the world, we never waited in line at clubs, never paid for a drink, and rarely returned home before the sun came up.

All this bonding and research led Julia Stiles, Sean Patrick Thomas, Fredro Starr, and me to rewrite a lot of the dialogue as we searched for our own authentic rhythms, just as we had been invited to do on *Our Song*.

The result was a film that was, and still is, beloved by audiences. It broke records for February box office numbers, even in the midst of a blizzard that ran up and down the East Coast on opening weekend. Chenille became an iconic character and a voice for Black women — still today, people quote her lines to me on the street and on social media. So much of our Black humanity is reduced to a statistic, but I was proud that I got to make Chenille, an African American teen mom from the inner city, not just an accessory to the lead character's story, but a fully human character in her own right.

~~~

The back-to-back releases of *Our Song* and *Save the Last Dance* were a crazy one-two punch. But despite having two highly successful projects — one, an art house independent film, and the other a big studio commercial hit — I was still working at a restaurant, substitute teaching in New York City Public Schools, and teaching yoga. I always made sure to have secondary sources of income because I would rather have worked extra shifts on a day job than have done a movie that felt disparaging to women or people of color. It meant that when I came across a script that I felt reinforced negative stereotypes,

I had a handful of other jobs to sustain me and maintain my creative freedom.

However, after *Save the Last Dance* came out, the vice principal at my favorite high school to teach at called me to his office.

"We love having you here," he said, "but kids are cutting class to catch a glimpse of you, to see Chenille. Perhaps you should stick to early elementary grades from now on...."

But teaching early elementary students came with its own challenges. If I found myself in a classroom for more than three days in a row, I would start to develop an attachment to the students. Maybe because of the teacher shortage in New York City, or maybe because I spent my entire childhood watching my mother teach teachers how to teach elementary students, invariably I would be offered a full-time teaching position. And if I had been with a class for more than three days, my love for those students, combined with the seduction of salaried work with benefits—not to mention guaranteed summers off— would feel almost impossible to resist. So, to preserve clarity and focus on my dreams of becoming a professional actor, I instituted a rule that I wouldn't work in the same classroom more than three days in a row.

~~∽~~

My first time playing the lead in a film—being number one on the call sheet—came the same year that *Save the Last Dance* was released. The character was Niecy, in a movie called *Lift*, and she was the consummate shoplifter in an intimate family drama disguised as an urban heist thriller.

There was a lot about Niecy that I understood and related to—her fashion sensibility, her class fluency, her ambition. But, Niecy was also a "booster," and other than a mid-century guide to etiquette for young women, and the odd snack from Park Avenue Spence girls' overstuffed refrigerators, I'd never stolen a thing. Wondering if I would be able to understand the adrenaline and excitement that was written into Niecy's relationship with theft, my directors—Khari Streeter and DeMane Davis—asked me if I'd ever stolen anything in real life. I quietly admitted that I hadn't while resolving to myself that I would.

I was terrified, but I was also determined. I needed to know what it was like to get away with something—I had to feel it inside my body, feel how my heartbeat changed, how my breathing quickened, how my palms got sweaty—so that I could incorporate those physical reactions into my portrayal of Niecy.

After much consideration and thorough location scouting, I chose a deli in Manhattan, just north of Times Square. But this was not a local library—this was a commercial place of business, with cameras and mirrors and, in my imagination, a big red button by the register that led directly to the local NYPD precinct. There was no way I was going to steal something with a tag or an alarm on it—I needed the lowest stakes possible. So, I would steal something that I could easily hide, exit the crime scene, and then dispose of the evidence in the most complete way possible.

I cased the joint two days in a row, studying the position of the security cameras, noting shift changes for various employees. I bought small items each day so that they would remember me as a customer in good standing. As I prepared for my crime, I knew, as did Niecy in the film, that the chances of being caught stealing were exponentially greater for me as a Black person because of the ways in which we are systemically mistrusted and surveilled.

All this for a Granny Smith.

The object of my thievery was in a bin with lots of other apples. I waited anxiously for the cashier to be distracted, slipped the apple into my tote bag, and sauntered out, pausing to appear calm and casual while glancing nonchalantly at the roasted almond display before exiting the front door.

I got it—not just the apple, but the real-life thrill that came from getting away with something illicit. Having rehearsed my getaway, I knew exactly where on Broadway I was no longer in sight of anyone working in the store, and when I reached that spot on the sidewalk, I started to run—partly to create as much distance between myself and the scene of the crime, but also because of the adrenaline that was coursing through me. The act of stealing was exhilarating, an unexpected pleasure. I'd already decided that if I'd been caught, I would have just pretended it was an accident. I wasn't going to blame the movie—that would have been a cop-out. But I'd gotten away with my crime and had been given new understanding of how to play Niecy.

With pride, I called the directors and told them what I'd done, offering to bring the apple to them as proof. They told me they believed me and to enjoy my bounty.

So, I ate it.

When the film wrapped, I went back to that same deli, bought a handful of snacks, offered more cash than was needed, and told the cashier to keep the change. It was my way of repaying my debt without admitting to my crime.

But my research didn't end there.

To understand the complicated relationship between Niecy and her mother, played by the legendary Lonette McKee, Khari and DeMane urged me to watch *Ordinary People*, the 1980 Robert Redford movie about the relationship between a mother and son, and to read Nancy Friday's classic book, *My Mother/My Self.*

Back during therapy in college, I'd mostly focused on my relationship with my dad and never had reason to discuss my mom. I wasn't aware that I had issues to work out with my mother. But watching *Ordinary People,* reading *My Mother/ My Self,* and working on *Lift* helped bring issues with my mother into focus. Niecy and her mom were caught in a cycle of enmeshment, where she was willing to do almost anything to please and be accepted by her mother. Playing her was giving me insight and illuminating something profound. While the dynamic wasn't precisely the same, I started to become aware of my own need to earn the love of a sometimes emotionally unavailable mother.

Like me, Niecy was a performer, willing to play the role that best offered security in her relationships. And in the life of a booster, that meant she also had to dress the part. She walked in the world like a wealthy young woman and pretended to belong in a socioeconomic environment that was not her own, an experience I understood firsthand from my years attending Spence.

We filmed *Lift* on a tight independent budget over the course of two months in Boston. It was my third feature film, and my second to premiere at Sundance, again to glowing reviews. The film was eventually bought by Showtime, and in 2001, I was nominated for an Independent Spirit Award for my portrayal of Niecy.

I hadn't gotten the nomination by wanting to be the "best" and win a prize. I knew that the recognition had instead come because I'd done the actor's homework of asking, "Who is Niecy? What does she want? What does she think? How does she feel?" By the end of *Lift*, Niecy learns that she cannot spend her life seeking her mother's approval, that her life must be her own. In asking those questions, I had discovered who Niecy was, but I'd also learned a lot about myself.

Being an actor is a great blessing because you get to step into a character, usually at the most pivotal points in their life— you learn their biggest lessons, integrate them into your own understanding, and, if you're lucky, move on to another character in another transformative moment. This means you, as the actor, get to evolve through the characters if you let them teach you.

It was as if these women, these powerful characters, were each trying to teach me something. They were like waking dreams coming through my subconscious. And because I struggled with fully understanding myself, my learning came through these characters, tiny miracles in the pursuit of my own awakening.

Eventually I would begin to ask those same questions of myself. I would learn to give myself the love and dignity that I bestowed upon my characters, to give myself permission to exist, to live, to be real, to take up space, and to matter.

But first, like Niecy, I had to leave the nest.

CHAPTER TEN

BLACK FAMOUS

When my mother dropped me at nursery school for my first day of pre-K, I barely flashed a look back. She has since said that witnessing my desire for independence at such a young age forced her to prepare for the inevitable day that I'd leave for college. In many ways, this safeguarding of her heart maintained the veil between us while also generously giving me the space to grow. Similarly, even though she didn't want me to pursue a professional career as an actor, she's always been supportive of me as an artist.

In 2003 I shot a movie directed by Spike Lee called *She Hate Me*. I played Fatima Goodrich, a lesbian who wants to bear a child and coerces her former fiancé to donate his sperm, which she uses to conceive. To act out the birthing scene, I wanted to know more about my mother's experience giving birth to me, so I called her one day from the hair and makeup trailer to ask about the night that I was born. (I know for many people this is a story that gets told throughout their childhood, but for some reason my origin story was a mystery to me.)

At first, my mother seemed surprised by my request, then I could almost hear her impulse to withhold—it was a silence I knew well. But then, without any reason I could discern, she dove in.

Her story began four weeks before my birth. In the weeks leading up to my birthday—the final day of January—there was a winter storm every Friday, and Fridays just happened to be when her ob-gyn appointments were scheduled. On one particular Friday, with contractions just beginning, her doctors told her to skip the appointment, as another storm was coming, but by Sunday she knew she had to go to the hospital.

I was born on the night the final episode of *Roots* aired (January 30, 1977)—well, 1:44 a.m. the next day, to be precise. My dad is such a lover of cinematic narrative and the excitement of a shared experience that my mother found herself alone with her doctor in the delivery room because my dad had convinced the nursing staff to watch the show with him in the waiting room. Legend has it that he was so moved by the *Roots* finale that when he returned, he wanted to change their plan from calling me Kerry Marisa Washington to naming me after one of the characters in the show, but my mother refused. (We still joke that I was almost Kunta Kinte Washington, but I don't know what name from *Roots* he'd actually pitched.)

Before that night, a lot of thought had gone into the name they had chosen. My parents hadn't known the gender of their child and, being as committed to austerity as my mother is, not to mention slightly ahead of her time, she wanted a gender-neutral name that could fit a baby boy or girl. In the seventies many Black Americans were giving their children Afrocentric names to honor and celebrate our lineage. But my mother wanted to find a name that embraced her pride in being a Black woman, while also honoring her mixed heritage. She knew that her family was descended from Scottish and Irish immigrants (legend had it they were pirates) who had landed in Jamaica and settled there, and in her research, she'd learned that Kerry means "little dark one" in Irish, in reference to the southern areas of Ireland where the landscape and people are rich in darker tones. (Specifically, Kerry was originally Chiar-raí; "ciar" means black, or sometimes dark-haired. The "Black Irish" are generally from County Kerry.)

On that call she talked about holding me for the first time; the look of pride in my dad's eyes and the relief she felt when I cried. I wondered if that relief was juxtaposed with the grief of her stillborn child, who had been cruelly whisked away from her years before.

I could feel how hard it was for her to tell me this story. I felt like she was tiptoeing with me through a field of land mines but was determined to get to the other side. I blamed the ghost of my stillborn sibling. *Perhaps,* I thought, *she couldn't relay the joy of my birth without revisiting the depths of that loss.* But I was so grateful for even the tiptoe because in that brief account she had given me more of my origin story than I'd ever had before, and it unlocked a deep well of emotion that I brought with me when it was my turn to labor and perform an imaginary birth. When I watched that moment of the film for the first time, I saw a character becoming a mother, awash in emotions that had all been gifted to me by my mother.

However, what my parents saw when they attended the premiere of *She Hate Me* was memorable for other reasons. A few days before, I'd sat them down to warn them about some of the graphic scenes they were about to witness.

"Just so you know, there's a lot of sex in this movie," I said, summoning up all the fake bravado I could muster and using the most graphic language I could imagine. "You're going to see me have rough sex with a guy, standing up against a wall; and also me getting finger-fucked on a kitchen counter by my girlfriend."

Ever since my days with S.T.A.R., I'd been testing my boundaries with them, pushing against the limits of what I thought was appropriate. They had learned by this point that the only appropriate response was to meet my false bravado with a fake nonchalance.

"Got it," my mother said as my dad guffawed.

It was January in New York City; I'll never forget how cold it was that morning. I was grateful for the need of additional layers, not only to keep me warm, but to hide in and cocoon myself away from the reality of the procedure I was about to undergo. Years after my mother had ventured into the cold as an act of maternal devotion, I was now attempting the opposite.

I sat in the waiting room and completed the paperwork with false data: a made-up name, a pretend address, a nonexistent email. Only the phone number was my own, should the office need to reach me in case of an emergency.

I remember looking around the room and wondering about the circumstances of the other women there. *Were they pregnant, too? Did they want to be? Were they wondering the same about me?* Afraid that they might be, I used my scarf to hide myself further. I was not, at this time, famous. I was a working actor, someone able to pay my rent and my car insurance. I had been in a few magazines, and my star was on the rise. But my work had not become an impediment to how I traveled through the world. Still, I wanted to be careful, wanted this procedure to remain private.

When the nurse called my false name, I followed her into a small office. She proceeded to ask me questions that she was required to ask by the state, to help me make sure that this was the right choice for me "and my family." My body felt hot with shame. As a health educator, I had spent so many years on the other side of a version of that conversation, asking young people to consider their options and weigh the consequences. I was schooled, and schooled others, in the ways of prevention and the language of sexual empowerment, but in my own life I had committed the crime that seemed unimaginable to me as a teenager. I had let my discomfort with communicating my feelings dictate choices that would impact me for a lifetime.

And now I was sitting across from a nurse, having to defend my desire to have an abortion. She reminded me of myself—we seemed to be about the same age; she too was a Black woman who I imagined had grown up in the outer boroughs of New York City. I answered her questions calmly and succinctly. Her lingering gaze told me that she was unaccustomed to such highly prepared patients.

Later, as I lay on the medical bed with my feet in stirrups, the doctor described her plans for the termination, the instruments she would be using, and what it might feel like at different stages along the way. I had been to several gynecological appointments through the years, but never one so transactional. Today I had come to this office for a particular result and required a definitive outcome. When I left, I would be a changed woman, without the burden of new life, but perhaps with a bit more time to understand and define my own.

Why hadn't I protected myself? Why hadn't I had the courage to create boundaries around my womb? Why had I silenced my preferences in the name of people-pleasing?

This all could have been avoided. If I had spoken up for myself in the moment, I wouldn't have found myself in that office. But there I was, surrendering my insides to a surgical vacuum, trying to repair the damage born of my silence and need to be loved.

Both the doctor and the nurse treated me with great kindness and care, as the website had promised. I was doing my best to breathe through the procedure and remain calm until it was over. And then, the nurse—the same nurse who had spoken with me before the abortion—let her eyes linger on me once more. She seemed to be trying to solve a problem. As the doctor opened my cervix and inserted the thin vacuum tube, the nurse looked down at me, smiled, and very gently said, "Do you know who you look like?"

I think she was trying to comfort me, to tell me that even though this moment was incredibly difficult, she could see the beauty in me, could see that I reminded her of a movie star, someone she appeared to like a great deal.

She said my name, my real name. I could hear it under the muffled sound of the water in which I was drowning.

My real name, right there in that room. Right there in that moment, as I was offering what could have been my future child into an abyss of futurelessness. She said that I looked like Kerry Washington. That girl from the movies. That girl from the magazines. It was my name, but the version she was calling out had nothing to do with me. And so, in that moment, I didn't know who I was. Or where I stood.

I only knew that my name belonged to public spaces in a way that made privacy unavailable to me.

~~~

For all my fledgling successes, if I was going to take my career to the next level, I was going to have to move west. I was already chafing at New York. After living in India, I'd moved back in with my parents, into the same room where I'd been brought home from the hospital. Now, with some movies under my belt—and appearances on all three different iterations of *Law & Order*—I wanted to get my own place, but I got the sense that my dad especially didn't want me to leave.

When he doesn't like the reality of change, my dad turns away from it, ignores it, and denies it. For a while I'd been crashing at a place that belonged to a friend of a friend, an old Hell's Kitchen apartment with a small loft bed and a bathtub in the kitchen that doubled as a dining room table when covered by a six-by-three plank of plywood. This situation, although a tiny paradise to me, was devastating to my parents. My mother's parents had risen out of the poverty of New York tenements, only for my parents to see me choose to go back in.

I wasn't speaking to my dad at the time because even though he was a licensed real estate broker, he wouldn't help me find a place of my own. Eventually, I did find a place in East Harlem through the classified ads in the *New York Daily News*. My roommate was my childhood friend, Kyana—she was a poet, actress, and musician, and was one of my earliest friends, given that our mothers had been members of a women's circle in the seventies when they had been pregnant with us. My dad refused to guarantee the apartment, which caused a huge fight between us (my mom cosigned the lease in the end). Looking back, I wonder if he did what he thought was best, thinking that my mother might be the one whose accounts reflected more financial stability.

I loved that first apartment; it became a haven for a rotating cast of young creatives. We would pool our meager resources, have potluck gatherings, hold *The Artist's Way* study groups, and nurture one another's dreams. There were friends from college, friends from S.T.A.R. theater, all at different stages of our fledgling careers. I was working multiple jobs, auditioning, and taking acting classes; Kyana was writing, painting, performing, and developing her craft; others were a bit further along, like our friend Miles, who was already years into his tenure as one of the company members of *Stomp*, both off-Broadway and on their international tours.

But as my career progressed, it became clear that the center of employment for film and television was Los Angeles. And I was ready to make that leap.

Again, I was asking my parents to support my adventures into the unknown, and this time they both did so, lovingly. My dad was particularly proud of my quest and kept affirming his belief in my version of a manifest destiny ("Go west, young man!" he'd say, jokingly).

Once in LA, I'd decided to ditch the extra jobs I'd always had and just focus on acting. I'd saved enough money leading up to the move that by the time I got to LA I was able to spend most of my time auditioning, taking acting classes, and reading scripts. (I was also lucky that a dear friend and producer, Dave Leyrer, lent me a temporary place to stay and a car to drive.) And when I wasn't engaged in my craft, I was spending hours in one-on-one and group therapy sessions as I continued to unravel the issues surrounding my compulsive relationship with food, exercise, and body image.

In both work and life, I was trying to break free, to go beyond the labels and limitations of who I'd been up to this point. In 2004, I appeared in a film called *Against the Ropes*, starring Meg Ryan and Omar Epps. In it, I played Meg's coworker and confidante—this was becoming a new niche for me, the white girl's best friend. It had started with *Save the Last Dance* and extended to a role on a TV pilot called *Wonderfalls*. *When Harry Met Sally* is, to this day, one of my three favorite movies of all time, so once I'd played Meg Ryan's best friend, playing the role against anyone else would have been a lateral move. I made the decision to stop there.

I wanted to reach for something more substantive; I wanted to be the lead. I decided to take a leap and pursue roles as a "leading lady." It's not that I wanted to be the star of the film; I wanted my characters to be in a story of their own. I didn't want to be an accessory to a white woman's journey. I wanted to play women with agency who were living through pivotal moments of their own, not just helping lead characters reflect on their "protagonistic" journeys.

This began an exciting period of my career in which I played opposite several of Hollywood's most esteemed Black actors and comedians, from Chris Rock to Don Cheadle to Eddie Murphy to Samuel L. Jackson to the Wayans brothers. And also something magical happened: in two extraordinary films I had the honor of playing the wife opposite brilliant actors who both went on to win Academy Awards for their portrayals.

~~~

The script for *Ray* had been circulating around town and there was a lot of buzz. Rumor had it that the screenplay, which was to be directed by Taylor Hackford, was a masterful biopic, filled with music and history and captivating emotional turbulence.

There were many important women in Ray Charles's life, from his mother to his wives to the women that he toured with, some of whom he was also romantically involved with. This meant that the script was not only a potential tour de force for its lead actor, Jamie Foxx, but also included tremendous acting opportunities for several Black female actors.

I was asked to read for the role of Della Bea Robinson, Ray Charles's wife. In my callback audition, I was asked to read with Jamie Foxx, who was already cast in the role of Ray. What followed was a full-on, old-school Hollywood screen test, replete with costumes, lights, hair and makeup, and film cameras instead of the camcorders that were usually used to film auditions.

I wanted to do everything I could to get the part, and I'd read in celebrity profiles in glossy fashion magazines that female movie stars often brought baked goods to the set, so that's what I did for the screen test. I baked chocolate chip cookies and brought them in a tin to share with the crew—amusingly, in my later research, I would learn that Della Bea was actually a terrible baker, but apparently my cookies were great, because I got the part.

～～

Ray marked Jamie Foxx's transition into becoming a serious film actor. He was a star already, of course—he had done *In Living Color,* and *The Jamie Foxx Show,* his sitcom, had run for years. He'd appeared in *Ali* and *Any Given Sunday,* and had released hit comedy specials. He'd already played important supporting characters, but with Ray, it was clear that this would be his breakout.

When my manager, Kathy, called me to ask me how it was going, I said, "Jamie Foxx is either doing a spot-on impersonation, or I'm witnessing an Academy Award–winning performance."

Jamie is one of the most wonderful lead actors I have ever had the privilege to work with. On a film set, every actor is assigned a number based on the importance of the character they're playing, and being number one on the call sheet comes with a certain implied responsibility to the film and to the community of artists and artisans working to make it. Years later, on the set of *Scandal*, whenever anybody complimented me on my leadership skills as a number one on the call sheet, I was always sure to credit Jamie for setting the best possible example. Both on-screen and off, Jamie is invested in bringing out the best in everyone around him. His generosity, it seems, has no limits.

This was evident from our very first day of filming. In preparation for the role, I had dedicated myself to perfecting a southern accent, because I'd never done accent work before, and Della Bea was from Richmond, Texas. At the end of the rehearsal of the first scene we shot together—the one in which Ray teaches Della Bea to listen for the sound of a hummingbird outside the window—Jamie said to me, "I can tell how much work you've put into the accent." (Jamie is from Texas.) "But I can see you thinking about it. Now you need to let it go." He could tell that thinking about my accent was limiting my ability to get lost in the scene.

When watching the film today, my self-consciousness about the accent can be interpreted as my character's insecurity because it's our first date. Della Bea was not yet entirely comfortable with Ray, and I was not yet entirely comfortable with Della Bea. But in the scene you can see two actors building rapport and history and intimacy. I was learning to trust Jamie, and Jamie was helping me to trust myself.

Months later, we shot the scene in the film in which Della Bea finds Ray's "works"—his heroin paraphernalia—for the first time. We filmed the scene in a small bathroom and up and down the stairway of a modest house in New Orleans. Early that morning, I felt that we had captured an exciting level of fear and frenzy, and it was exhilarating. Scenes that engender that kind of heightened emotion can be intoxicating, and sometimes, in the pursuit of that high, I have found myself doing the same thing over and over again, in this case trying to manufacture the same levels of shock, disappointment, and disapproval in every take.

But you can't create more magic with mere repetition. You have to keep inviting it and stirring the pot and poking the bear and whispering to the magic and remaining open to a response. The one thing you can't do is to push the same button again and again.

By the afternoon, as we continued to work on this particular scene because I wasn't surrendering to the magic, I found myself trying to force it. I felt that I just couldn't get to where I wanted to go emotionally; I couldn't find the truth. It was as if I were merely performing an idea of the scene. I had never been on a movie this big, or had this important a role, and I knew I wasn't getting it right.

Jamie recognized that I was abandoning the unpredictability of truth by trying to do the scene the same way, over and over again.

"Keep searching," he said. He swung his head toward me but couldn't look at me directly because his eyes were covered by prosthetics that prevented him from seeing. "You have to let it be different every time. Don't try to make it be what it was just keep finding new things. Play..."

I knew he was right—I hadn't been in flow, I hadn't lost myself in the truth of the scene as I had that morning. But Jamie's advice meant that I didn't have to go backward. I could go forward; I could keep searching ahead for the truth.

With that new approach, the scene began to sing. I asked myself, "What new moment can I discover? What new item can I find in his bag of works? How can I respond to him differently?" This felt like freedom.

Jamie had thrown me a lifeline. People-pleasing and perfectionism were still signature parts of my personality—the shape-shifting I'd learned as a child had created in me a desire to get it "right" instead of digging for the unknown. I was trying to embody somebody else's idea of who a character or what a scene was supposed to be...who *I* was supposed to be, in fact.

With Jamie's help I remembered that acting was about discovery, about messy, flawed humanity, and about being open to something new each and every time, not about being perfect or doing the same thing twenty times in a row.

~~

Once we'd finished filming *Ray*, Universal Studios bought the distribution rights to the film but held on to it for most of a year. At the time, this was frustrating; by all accounts the film was special, filled with tremendous performances. I was proud of the work I had done, and I wanted the movie to be out in the world, partly because I hoped that it would lead to more work.

But Universal, I learned, had a bigger plan. This was an awards contender, and movies that win Oscars typically come out at the end of a year so that members of the Academy have the films seared into their recent memory when it's time to vote the following January.

So, in the fall of 2004, *Ray* premiered to rave reviews and a standing ovation at the Toronto International Film Festival. Suddenly I felt like I was at the center of a whirlwind. It was how I imagine it would feel to be shot out of a cannon— a blinding flash of heat, and an onslaught of immediate fame. The buzz was everywhere; the press corps was insatiable. Jamie was positioned as an Oscar contender, as was the film, and we were all suddenly in a race. I had heard people refer to "Oscar races" in the past, but now I understood: the process involved all the political necessities of a run for national office, with the competitive requirements needed for a sprint toward Olympic gold.

Little by little I started to learn the language around this culture of campaigning. *Ray* would become the film that introduced me to Oscar parties and the Golden Globes. There would be "gifting suites," profile pieces in print media, and primetime interviews, "For Your Consideration" billboards and full-page ads in the trade magazines. Seemingly endless panel discussions and Q and As with every guild imaginable and film festivals strategically held in cities where Oscar voters lived.

One night I was lying down in the back seat of a car, coming home from a screening at the Palm Springs International Film Festival. There were two producers up front, and as they were chatting, one of them said, referring to me, "I think she has a shot at Best Supporting..." I'd been in and out of sleep for most of the ride but had heard that. I wished I hadn't—it made me immediately anxious because I felt the pressure to please and achieve. I felt that now there were expectations for me to be something other than an artist. Now, I had to be a winner... now I had to be in the race.

I didn't want to put my artistry in a horse race. Partly because I didn't think I could win. But I also didn't want to lose, I didn't want to fail, I didn't want to disappoint people. I dreaded having the feelings I imagine my dad had struggled with when his business ventures failed.

I also got cynical. Knowing that there was a culture of campaigning for these awards allowed me a peek behind the curtain that fractured any concept of "best" in the creative arts. Campaigns were built to increase popularity and win votes. I would argue that one doesn't win these kinds of awards without tremendous talent and the work to show for it, but it was also now clear to me why some of the greatest performances of our time had not been awarded trophies. The award doesn't always go to the "best" performance—it goes to one of the year's most extraordinary performances backed up by an effective campaign.

Even without Universal's superb strategy, Jamie's brilliant performance would have easily earned him Best Actor at the Academy Awards, as well as a BAFTA and a Golden Globe. Taylor would be nominated for Best Picture and Best Director, but despite the buzz around several of the supporting performances by women in the film—Regina King, Aunjanue Ellis, Sharon Warren, and me—none of us would receive an Academy Award nomination. There was a theory that our performances may have cannibalized each other by splitting the vote.

Nonetheless, each of us benefited from the glow of being part of an Oscar-nominated film. The press surrounding *Ray* led to my first magazine cover—*Essence*, where Jamie stood between Regina King and me. While it was thrilling to be shooting my first cover, what I remember most was guilt about the absence of Aunjanue and Sharon, and resistance to standing at the front of the pack.

With this cover shoot, I had a new excuse to engage in dangerous old patterns. In preparing for the shoot, my perfectionism went into overdrive. I prepped, and coiffed, and severely limited my food intake to try to control the image that would appear on newsstands and my fears surrounding that. My heightened success only seemed to justify the resurgence of these old demons.

In the midst of navigating new levels of opportunity, success, and public recognition, another private matter eclipsed it all: my mother reluctantly shared with me that she had been diagnosed with breast cancer. They had caught it early, so she had been able to avoid chemotherapy, but she'd undergone both a biopsy and a course of radiation. She had wanted to protect me from the pain of the unknown, and, as was our tradition when it came to difficult truths, she had avoided sharing these details as they had unfolded, choosing only to tell me once her treatment was complete and her prognosis positive.

Now it was my turn to withhold truths. I told her that it was fine that she hadn't told me, but it wasn't. Inside, I felt even further adrift.

~~~

The first time I saw Forest Whitaker I was fifteen years old, sitting in a movie theater with my mother, watching *The Crying Game.* In that film, Forest Whitaker played a British soldier, and he was spectacular. Then, in 1995, he stole my heart completely when he directed the film adaptation of *Waiting to*

Exhale, a veritable love letter to Black women that remains an iconic film about Black female friendship.

I had the great pleasure of working alongside Forest Whitaker when I played Kay Amin in *The Last King of Scotland.* I had met Forest during the promotional whirlwind for *Ray* and was struck by his gentle warmth and sensitivity. But I never saw that gentle Forest Whitaker the whole time I was in Uganda. He'd disappeared, and in his place stood despot and military dictator Idi Amin.

Forest's complete transformation into the character was not without its dangers. At one point during the making of the movie, a journalist from the *Los Angeles Times* was slated to come to Uganda to write about the making of the film. This terrified producers, because Forest was so deeply committed to the embodiment of his character, even off set, that in his mind, Idi Amin was not a villain—he was a complicated and charismatic human being that Forest had been tasked to bring to life. For the historical record, Idi Amin was called all of these things at some point in his life: the Butcher of Kampala, the Butcher of Uganda, the Butcher of Africa, and the Black Hitler— he called *himself* "His Excellency, President for Life, Field Marshal Al Hadji Doctor Idi Amin Dada, VC, DSO, MC, CBE, Lord of All the Beasts of the Earth and Fishes of the Seas and Conqueror of the British Empire in Africa in General and Uganda in Particular."

Everyone in Uganda has a personal story about the reign of Amin. At one point, while I was being driven to set, I asked why we weren't driving down a street that seemed like a more direct route. The driver replied reluctantly, "My mother was killed on that street."

~~~

In *The Last King of Scotland*, I would play Kay, Amin's fourth wife. Despite the difficult emotional subject matter, it was wonderful to once again be on a project I could pour myself into.

When I got the role of Kay it was my first straight offer—meaning I didn't have to audition for the film—which to my mind was insane. For a start, I had no idea how to even begin to do a Ugandan accent. I thought our director, Kevin Macdonald, was crazy for trusting me to be able to do so, but I was a huge fan of two of his previous movies—the documentary *One Day in September*, about the 1972 Munich Olympics attack, and *Touching the Void*, a docudrama about a mountaineering accident. So, when we met in Los Angeles, I kept my doubts to myself.

Kay shares a passionate love affair with a Scottish doctor, played by James McAvoy. The affair leads to the conception and subsequent botched abortion of a child, from which Kay dies (she is then disemboweled by Amin's soldiers on his orders). In real life, Kay's lover was thought to be a Ugandan doctor—not the Scottish protagonist of our film—but the affair, abortion, death, and disembowelment were all true to history.

Filming began in Kampala, Uganda, in June 2005. Before leaving, I began working with legendary dialect coach Robert

Easton, because that's who Forest Whitaker was working with. I felt that it was important to be consistent with Forest's approach to the accent so that if we got anything wrong, at least we'd be getting it wrong together.

This was my first time visiting the continent of Africa. I wondered what it would feel like to be there, if I would discover a clearer sense of myself, and experience the belonging I'd been searching for. I knew from my time in India how powerful it could be to study, work, and live in a place surrounded by people who looked like me. But, as it might be for most African Americans, the continent of Africa was different—it held the promise of potentially finding answers to questions about my unknown beginnings.

Africa is where my ancestors are originally from, but the brutality of the transatlantic slave trade—the separation of families, and the attack on humanity through the forced erasure of names, languages, and customs—prevents me from knowing where exactly on the continent my family tree begins. That lack of firm understanding of who we are is a universal truth for Black people in the diaspora. Still, Africa, we are taught, is our motherland, and I wondered if she would embrace me.

It was not an auspicious beginning. When I landed at Entebbe, my bags did not land with me—they had not made it to my connecting flight. This meant that I faced at least twenty-four hours in Kampala with just the clothes on my back and a carry-on containing my script and a handful of American fashion magazines, as well as the pj's, the itchy socks, and the little airline toothbrush they'd handed out before we'd taken off.

A press conference had been scheduled for that first day, so I was thrust into an instant Ugandan experience: with members of our local production crew, I headed to a market to find something to wear. Showing up in the latest Kampala trends seemed to endear me to the local journalists and began to quickly erode the distance between Kerry Washington and Kay Amin. My job was to become a Ugandan woman. Being stripped of my personal belongings was an immediate invitation into this new culture and identity.

I was heading to Africa to become African—I wasn't playing an American character in Africa—so the lost luggage enabled me to arrive humbled, with my student mind and my anthropological lens activated. I was not Kerry Washington walking red carpets for summer blockbuster movies—in fact, filming in Uganda required that I miss the world premiere for *Mr. and Mrs. Smith*. I was once again that hungry artist on the A train shooting *Our Song*, grateful to be exactly where I was meant to be; and I was that student in India, awakened by the sights and sounds of a new culture, a social scientist in the field, saying "Teach me everything, take me everywhere."

Forest and I spent hours sitting outdoors, wanting to transform into darker hues of ourselves as we might have, were we living under that native sun. And in the evening, I found a circle of Ugandan women with whom I could spend my time. We met when the hair and makeup department referred a local woman to braid my hair for the film. She became an ambassador, a translator, and a touchstone. Disappearing into her world, and the world of her friends, helped me to find the accent, movements, and rhythms typical of Ugandan women. Hungry for the embrace of their sisterhood, and craving deep authenticity for the character of Kay Amin, I stopped speaking with an American accent while I was there, and instead always spoke with the musicality of the Ugandan lilt.

It was now clearer than ever that this disappearance of myself, the untethering of my reality into the imaginary in the service of a character, was one of the things I loved most about acting. By the time I was making *The Last King of Scotland*, I saw myself as a working character actor. I was not a household name. Few people made the connection that Kerry Washington was the same actor in such disparate films as *Save the Last Dance, She Hate Me*, and *Ray*. And each of these films attracted an entirely different core audience. If I was at all famous, I was what some of us in the business call "Black Famous." I had amassed enough work in the industry to gain the attention and respect of the film-loving members of my community, like that one kindhearted nurse at the abortion clinic. But in the culture at large, I was able to have a thriving career while remaining relatively anonymous.

The character of Kay is found mostly at the center of a tragic love story. The brutality of Kay's ending is what so many remember about that movie, but the scene in which Kay is standing in the shimmering waters of the pool at the Kampala Hilton, flirting with James McAvoy's character, is the one I think of the most. To me, Kay is a flesh-and-blood lover, not just a brutalized corpse. Her life is what I remember most, because through her I felt as though I'd had the privilege of swimming with my ancestors.

Once the movie came out and Forest won an Academy Award, I joked that I was becoming the actor who, if cast to play your wife, would help you win an Oscar.

I had worked with two of the best leading men in the business, the best number ones.

Next, it would be my turn.

CHAPTER ELEVEN

SUPERHEROES

I woke up the morning of Wednesday, November 9, 2016, and "Olivia Pope" was trending. All over Twitter people were saying, "Olivia Pope, you have to fix this," and "Olivia Pope, we need you to save the day."

By then I had spent five seasons playing the iconic political fixer on *Scandal,* and when I wasn't working, my attention was focused on my activism, my business interests, and most importantly, my marriage and my growing family.

The night before, with a heavy heart, I had stepped away from my mother and my husband and had gone to bed before the presidential election had been officially called. I couldn't bear thinking about my young children growing up in a country with that man as our commander in chief. But when I woke up in the middle of the night to nurse my son, I saw the inevitable news: a misogynistic, bankrupt white supremacist was to be the next president of the United States, and people wanted Olivia Pope to fix it.

This wasn't the first time that people on social media had evoked my character's name in response to a real political crisis. In the past, I had found it slightly amusing, but this morning was different. Millions of Americans had not voted; millions of people had chosen to give up their power and their voice, and now, here we were, caught on what many of us knew would be a terrifying road ahead. But instead of reflecting on the realities of how we got there, or on the realistic steps it would take to survive the nightmare that approached, we were calling on imaginary superheroes to save us.

A character from a reality TV show had become the president, and now people wanted a character from a primetime drama to somehow fix it — that is not how democracy works. I felt sick to my stomach.

~~~

In late 2007, I had been the subject of a photo essay for the *New York Times* style section that combined fashion with politics. Draped in looks fresh off the runway, I ran around Los Angeles with the team capturing images with candidates who were in town to woo voters ahead of the upcoming California Democratic primary. I had coffee with Dennis Kucinich and his wife, Elizabeth; shook hands with former New York City Mayor Rudolph Giuliani; greeted fans with New Mexico Governor Bill Richardson; and went to hear Barack Obama speak at the Universal Amphitheatre, where we had the opportunity to meet him for the first time.

I had become a fan of the then-senator when he spoke at the

2004 Democratic National Convention. I'd sat on my couch and watched him bring the convention to its feet with his rousing oratory and his groundbreaking vision for our country, and even then, I felt as though I was witnessing history.

Backstage at the amphitheater, I started to introduce myself, but he cut me off.

"I know who you are," Obama said. So, I quickly made sure to introduce him to the rest of our team, which included the then-fashion editor for the *Times*, Elizabeth Stewart. She and I caught eyes and silently agreed not to ask the senator to participate in the photo essay as we'd done with the other candidates. Many of them had been eager to be part of our story, but Obama's team seemed more focused on the authenticity of his message and his connection with his audience, rather than on the seduction of optics and the glamour of print media. We'd gotten photos of me standing with Obama's crowds at the amphitheatre — that was enough.

A few weeks later, as a board member of the Creative Coalition — an organization that advocates to protect federal funding for the arts and humanities — I was invited to attend the Democratic debate in South Carolina between Obama, then-senator Hillary Clinton, and former senator John Edwards. While there, I received news that a film I was slated to act in was going to be put on hold due to a writers' strike in Hollywood. With no urgent reason to return home, I accepted an invitation from the campaign to stay and participate in a fundraising event. As one of the more high-profile supporters in attendance, I was asked to say a few words. But I was slightly nervous given that I'd never worked on a campaign or spoken on behalf of a candidate before.

Claire McCaskill, then a freshman senator from Missouri, had made the bold decision to come forward as a woman in support of Obama rather than Clinton. I confided in her that I was anxious about speaking in front of this small crowd gathered in a living room somewhere near Myrtle Beach. Senator McCaskill told me that it was easier than it looked, that I just had to speak from my heart. She reassured me that as an actor, I would be just fine.

Then I watched her, and she was masterful. Her speech reminded me of a cross between an inspired lecture from a civics professor, a provocative monologue from a modern American play, and an intimate share from a group therapy meeting.

When it was my turn to speak, I knew exactly what to do.

For the next year, I was on and off the campaign trail, visiting sixteen states on behalf of the Obama campaign. I spoke at colleges, at community centers, in beauty shops and diners, in public parks, and at beach barbecues. On one Sunday morning in Tennessee, we visited four houses of worship before lunch. And when I had the opportunity to introduce my parents to Senator Barack Obama at the Congressional Black Caucus that year, my mother shook his hand and said, "Thank you for getting Kerry back into church."

What I saw in those sixteen states, many of which I'd never visited before, were people from different backgrounds all yearning for a country with more justice and equity and possibility for everyone. I saw people falling in love with

Obama's vision for a truly united country where, regardless of race, ethnicity, religion, sexual orientation, physical ability, or socioeconomic background, our humanity is valued and our voices matter. And I was becoming enchanted by the possibility of what America could become, as well as by the democratic process of how we could get there.

I loved being on the stump. I loved advocating for Barack and Michelle in the White House; but even more, I loved spending time in communities all over the country conveying to people how much they would matter to the Obama administration and how much they themselves mattered to me. I loved having people feel seen and heard and embraced by the political traditions of our democratic institutions. I loved reminding people that their votes mattered. That *they* mattered. And in some ways, devoting myself to that process and that mission helped me to feel like I mattered, too.

～〜～

My disordered relationship with my body had continued to evolve. I had good days and bad days. Structure, I learned, was important: setting boundaries and guidelines for myself based on what I'd learned in recovery about healthy eating and exercising habits proved to be helpful. When I could design a plan for food and exercise based on what I imagined my characters' habits might be, I found myself following them more consistently. Being able to show up physically for the characters I was being asked to embody, being able to eat and exercise according to the character's identity, being able to devote my body to their narrative, inspired in me a willingness to take better care of myself. Being these characters helped me to wrangle the compulsive voices within me.

But in between characters, I found myself more confused. I knew what was right for them but not for me. The loss of the character's lifestyle as my own produced a sense not only of mourning, but also of bewilderment. In some ways this wasn't entirely different from what actors who employ a "Method" approach to building out characters experience. But I knew that for me the choice was not just artistic—I had a desperate need to be directed toward "normal," healthy behavior, and the characters helped with that. Even if I imagined a character's food and exercise habits were not based on making the healthiest choices at all times, any structure that I could borrow from them was better than the chaos of being left to my own devices.

One role at a time, they were saving me.

But there was something else happening, too. With the loss of anonymity came increased concerns about not only how my body looked to me in the mirror, but also how it appeared on television, in movies, in fashion spreads, and on the covers of magazines. The day after a highly visible public appearance, or after the publication of new images, I would get ensnared in a wave of depression and anxiety. Increased publicity was seen by others as a good reason to celebrate my success, but locked in my bedroom, hiding under the covers, drowning in self-contempt, I would once again look to food and exercise to create a false sense of safety, as well as a kind of physical pain that mirrored the emotional swells I was trying to swim through.

It didn't matter that anyone wanted to put me in front of a camera or thought that the images were beautiful; it didn't matter what people said to me about my appearance — my brain was committed to the idea that I was not enough. Without the professional support of hair and makeup and wardrobe and the imaginary identity of a character to hide behind, I struggled to feel comfortable in my own skin. Left to myself, I didn't know how to eat as Kerry... or *be* as Kerry.

But that changed on the campaign trail. On the trail, there was no structure. We were in hotel rooms in different cities every single day. The food was unpredictable; whether we had access to a gym was a complete toss-up; there was no hair and makeup department, no wardrobe other than jeans and Obama T-shirts.

But I had found a new character to plug into, a new narrative. I was part of a team of people working together to tell a fresh story about America. I had become an official surrogate for the Obama campaign, an evangelist for hope and change and justice and democracy and belonging. I needed our country to be these things partly because I needed them for myself— but we all did. On the trail, I got to be in service to something bigger than myself, a national network, a global community working toward change. Even though this role required me to let go of structure and discipline and guidelines, I found comfort in the adventure of being on the stump. I escaped into the whirlwind, grateful for this new identity to hold on to, this fresh sense of purpose to anchor me and protect me from the voices that wanted me to believe I had nothing to offer. My obsession with food and exercise and my body weakened with my eyes turned outward to community building and civic engagement.

I wasn't rooted in supporting my scene partner or perfecting an imaginary character, but I was devoted to something other than myself. There was freedom in rejecting the need for control and perfectionism that had plagued me for so long.

~~~

To be an actor is to consider the humanity of others. It's my job to see the world through other people's eyes and to step into their shoes. To me, there's a connection between the craft of acting and a belief in the importance of human rights. My pull toward civic engagement is born of my understanding that each of us has a valuable perspective and important dreams for ourselves and our families and our future. Voting is an added expression of those values and beliefs. Each one of us matters and deserves to have our voices heard and our stories told, not just in entertaining content but through the representative bodies that guide the laws and rules of our lives.

So, in 2009, when Obama was sworn in as president and I was offered a role with the administration, I was deeply honored. Eventually I would I join the President's Committee on the Arts and the Humanities, a committee serving the presidency and cochaired by First Lady Michelle Obama.

As with all federal appointees, I had to endure a lengthy vetting process lasting almost a year. During that year, I landed the parts of Broomhilda von Shaft in Quentin Tarantino's *Django Unchained* and Olivia Pope on *Scandal*. But before auditioning for either, when the vetting process began I was performing in my first play on Broadway, originating the role of Susan in David Mamet's play, *Race*.

It was there at the Barrymore Theatre that I met Nnamdi Asomugha backstage. He was in New York to visit friends and indulge his love of theater, and given his importance at CAA— the agency that represented us both (him originally as an athlete; me as an actor)—they arranged for the cast to receive him and his sister Chisara backstage after the show. Later I would be reminded that although I'd never met Nnamdi before, he and I had cohosted a fundraiser in Northern California for Kamala Harris's attorney general campaign. We had both been unable to attend the event but had lent our names in support of what I was certain would be a stellar political career. But that night at the Barrymore, we finally did meet, and I felt dizzied by the calm and pure authenticity of his presence.

I still am.

~~

It was at lunch one day, sitting in my trailer in New Orleans while filming *Django,* that I realized I needed to call Valerie Jarrett, the president's most senior advisor.

"Valerie," I said, "I want to give you a heads-up about some acting projects I'm working on. Obviously, my role on the president's committee is an enormous priority and a tremendous honor, but I'm concerned that perhaps my day job might be a bit of a distraction in months to come."

Valerie asked me to explain.

"Well...," I said, "I just finished shooting a few episodes for a new network series where I play a high-profile DC fixer who happens to be having an affair with the president of the United States." I paused to let that sink in, and then added, "But don't worry, he's a Republican!"

Valerie laughed.

Then I said, "And right now, I'm in New Orleans shooting a big Tarantino film with Jamie Foxx, where we play escaped slaves who blow up the plantation at the end of the movie."

"Huh," Valerie said. And then, "Congratulations!"

"I know, I know," I said, in the tone of an apology. "I believe in these projects. I think they're both important. And I'm proud to be a part of them. But I would absolutely understand if my participation in this work would require me to resign from the committee. I wouldn't want the White House to be positioned as endorsing these themes in any way."

Valerie thanked me for calling her. She reassured me that I'd been invited to the committee because I was a brave artist and a bold advocate. She said she would talk to some folks and get back to me if there was an issue.

I remained on the committee, and I was proud of all we accomplished. We coauthored an investigative report with the Department of Education on the state of arts education around the country and its proven power to improve overall academic performance. And in the following years, our recommendations led to an initiative called Turnaround Arts aimed at transforming some of the most challenged schools in the country by boosting academic achievement and increasing student engagement through the use of "high-quality and integrated arts education." In the pilot phase of the program, I worked with Savoy Elementary School in Washington, DC, where I donated resources, gave workshops, and attended classes and performances; I would do the same in later years at Warren Lane Elementary School in Inglewood, CA.

～✼～

The pretend elevator doors slid open, and Oprah Winfrey walked down the hall of Olivia Pope & Associates on soundstage 5 of Sunset Gower Studios.

It was the second season of *Scandal,* and in episode after episode, new clients had entered my character's offices looking to be saved. But today I was sitting down at our enormous conference table, surrounded by glass walls, with one of my heroes.

Oprah was interviewing me for a new series called *Oprah's Next Chapter* on her network, OWN. I had been asked to appear once before on a different show, *Super Soul Sunday.* This was a show I loved and watched religiously, but on *Super Soul Sunday,* public figures would come on and talk about themselves, their spiritual and emotional journeys, and share their insight and wisdom. I declined that invitation, worried that I had little wisdom to offer, and fearing that the lingering disconnect I felt with myself meant that I was in no position to offer insight to others.

But *Oprah's Next Chapter* was different. Oprah wasn't coming to set to talk to me about my journey or my inner life. She was coming to talk about the work, and about my characters,

Olivia Pope on *Scandal*, and Broomhilda von Shaft in *Django Unchained*, which would soon be released. I couldn't have been more excited.

It had been a tremendous year. We'd shot *Django* in the nine months between filming seasons one and two of *Scandal*, and I'd had very little downtime in between. In fact, reshoots for the film took place on a weekend after I'd returned to work on *Scandal*. As I told Oprah in the interview, I was faced with the challenge of leaping two centuries in two days, going from playing a runaway slave chased barefoot through the woods by men with lanterns to playing a woman who was being referred to at the time as "the First Lady of Drama," a Dior-suited, Prada-purse-carrying powerhouse.

When *Scandal* first aired, a great deal of the press centered on the fact that at the time it had been thirty-seven years since a Black woman appeared as the lead of a network drama. Every Black woman in Hollywood auditioned for the role of Olivia Pope. We all knew that it was a historic, once-in-a-lifetime opportunity. For my audition, I worked with both the legendary acting coach Susan Batson and Colleen Basis, one of my best friends from college and the matron of honor at my wedding, who has gone on to be a brilliant acting coach, as well.

When the call came in that the role was mine, I was sitting in a booth at a Mexican restaurant in Manhattan Beach with my then-boyfriend, Nnamdi. Filled with gratitude and excitement, we walked down to the ocean after dinner, where we held each other under a benevolent moon and thanked God for the opportunities that lay ahead.

~∾~

Every interview that I did to promote *Scandal* talked not only about showrunner Shonda Rhimes's incredible writing, the fiery chemistry between Tony Goldwyn and me, our stellar ensemble of actors, and the unforgettable costumes designed by Lyn Paolo, but also about the history that was being made simply because I was number one on the call sheet.

Olivia Pope became an icon. For many Americans, she was the first Black woman they spent time with in their homes in an intimate way, week after week, for an hour at a time. For others, she was one of us—she represented a version of Black excellence that allowed us to see ourselves in our smartest and most powerful forms, perfectly coiffed, well-heeled, fearlessly at the center of power, and with an unimpeachable mastery of language. She was smart, she was beautiful, and she was messy. She was in full control within her crisis management firm, while also at the center of her tumultuous romance. She had been written to embody the complexity of being of a flawed human being and an antihero who remained an aspirational role model.

Olivia was complicated, she was human, and she had arrived.

So, when Oprah asked me what it was like to play her and Broomhilda in the same year, I shared the gratitude and responsibility I felt in having the opportunity to tell the story of these two women on opposite ends of freedom. Olivia was not perfect—where's the drama in that?—but in many ways she was the answer to Broomhilda's prayers. Aside from her moments of weakness with the president, she was the most powerful person in every room. While Broomhilda was running toward freedom, and toward a future where she would be considered a full human being, not three-fifths of a person, and where she would have the legal agency to live a life of independence and self-determination, Olivia Pope *was* that woman. She was the boss; her life was her own; and the only person she was running from was herself.

~~~

When I read the script for *Django Unchained*, I was terrified. I realized that it was groundbreaking, but there was much more explicit sexual violence in the draft I read than in anything I'd done before. But there were a number of reasons to take the role: for one, I loved the script and could not put it down. Also, I wanted to work with Tarantino. Like many actors, I wanted to work with the greats, and he was high on that list. I saw in the pages of the script that what Tarantino had done was turn a slave narrative about escape into an action-packed origin story of an antebellum superhero. At the heart of the film was a love story between Jamie Foxx's character and mine. I was thrilled at the opportunity to work with Jamie again and was moved by the importance of the romance between our characters.

Django and Broomhilda were two enslaved people who loved each other, but at that point in US history they would have been considered property and not human beings, and it was illegal for those of African descent to marry each other. To maintain the institution of chattel slavery, Black family members were routinely separated from one another without regard for romantic or familial relationships. And so, *Django Unchained* is a pre-Emancipation love story, the tale of a Black man who escapes enslavement, discovers his freedom, rescues the woman he loves, and avenges the abuses they had endured.

Still, the original script contained scenes where Broomhilda escaped abuse running naked down the street, and a terrifyingly brutal rape scene. I had done a great deal of negotiating before signing on to the film, especially about my nudity clause—I wanted there to be a lot less than what was originally written. And I'd gotten to a point where I felt comfortable enough to sign on for the role. I knew how important it was to tell this story and hoped that I could have a voice in the process and help to shape the scenes, so that the images in the film would adequately capture the devastations of slavery while not objectifying the lead characters or being salacious or gratuitous. During production several scenes were cut or rewritten, but scenes like the one in which my character is pulled naked from a torturous hotbox, or whipped on her bare back by her overseers, remained. If our mission was to tell the story of one couple's heroic journey out of slavery, despite all odds, we could not dilute the horror of what that enslavement entailed, especially since we were on sacred ground.

A great deal of the filming took place on an actual plantation—Evergreen Plantation in Edgard, Louisiana, near

New Orleans—and throughout the process, the cast and crew often felt we were communing with our ancestors, surrounded by ghosts. Many days, Jamie arranged with our sound department to have gospel music playing between takes, and there was a profound sense of reverence on set, a feeling of gratitude to our ancestors and awe at what they had survived. Our job as actors was to embody their unimaginable existence, and to do so we prayed for their strength and leaned into one another, grateful for friendship and an already established creative partnership.

On the night the rape scene was to be shot, I went to my trailer, put on my costume—a simple cotton nightgown—and placed a pillow from the couch of the mobile home onto the floor and kneeled to pray. I'd been praying all day for wisdom and insight, for some sense of direction on how to best serve the film. I'd been asking God to give me clarity about how much of the fear should be embraced as Broomhilda's instead of mine; how much of it was mine to overcome as an artist dedicated to my craft; and how much was appropriate and necessary to guide me toward advocating for what I believed was the best possible version of the scene.

When the knock came on my trailer door inviting me to set, I held on tight to the rosary I had chosen for Broomhilda that she kept with her always. I tried to steady my breath as I walked across the grounds of the plantation toward the tiny cabin where the scene was to take place. Once inside the room, I noticed the lights set up to emulate the flickering glow of flames. Jamie and Quentin stood in the corner; both men were looking down at the dirt floor, and as I walked toward them, Tarantino announced that we were all going home. The scene would be cut from the script.

Maybe it was something Jamie had said to Quentin in the days before that had finally seeped in. Maybe something shifted for Quentin standing in that cabin. Either way, it was the answer to the prayers I'd been whispering on my knees.

I think the movie is better for the absence of that scene, but even without it, there is no lack of brutality depicted. When Broomhilda is caught by overseers after an attempt to run away, there's a scene in which she's whipped. The scene was shot at the base of a majestic tree. We had historians on set to help support the authenticity and accuracy of the film, and at one point, one of our production assistants asked, "Why doesn't that tree have any moss?" And the historian said, "That was probably a hanging tree."

So, I knew in that moment, as we shot the scene in which Broomhilda was struggling to withstand her lashing, that I was standing on holy ground where someone like her, like me, had died. When I cried out in pain from the carefully choreographed beating, I was weeping for generations of enslaved people who had come before me and the realities of what they'd endured. And I felt humbled to be telling a version of their story that brought light to their humanity and honor to their love.

~~

One of the things I loved most about *Django* was that within the historical context of slavery, Jamie's character got to be a rescuing superhero prince, and I got to be a damsel in distress, a princess in a tower in a larger-than-life revenge quest. I knew at the time that waiting to be rescued from a tower was not a particularly feminist idea, but I also felt that as Black families, we were deserving of superheroes and fairy tales, too. So, the fight to be together in love, despite the larger system at play, became both a story of liberation and an overtly political act.

When my cousin John, who later became a visual artist, was in elementary school, he spent most of his spare time writing and illustrating his own comic books. He was obsessed with superheroes and their adventures. One afternoon, when I was still an infant, my dad asked John why he never drew any Black superheroes. And John said, "Because there aren't any."

My dad heard John's observation as an invitation and was determined in that moment to prove John wrong—to prove that there were superheroes in the world who looked like us. This was one of those moments where my dad's magic was undeniable.

"Have you never heard of Chitterlin' Man?" my dad said.

"No...," John said, confused.

"Oh!" my dad exclaimed. "Chitterlin' Man is *the* Black superhero. I'm friends with him. So maybe you guys could meet one day."

For the next twenty years, my dad would sometimes call John, disguising his voice and pretending to be Chitterlin'

Man. One year, for a fraternity masquerade ball, he dressed up as Chitterlin' Man, with a mask and a cape and a sidekick called Hot Sauce, who looked a lot like my mother. And on the day that John got married, he got a greeting card with some cash from Chitterlin' Man.

Because of my dad, John never again doubted the existence of Black superheroes. And neither did I.

CHAPTER TWELVE

FAMILY

The first time I saw the pilot of *Scandal,* Shonda had invited the cast to her house to watch it. We sat in her gorgeous open-plan living room, a place awash in creams and grays that felt like it had been ripped from the pages of *Architectural Digest.* The art on the walls was beautiful, the lighting elegant, and the bouquets freshly arranged. I had been in homes like this when I was at Spence, homes that felt somehow aspirational and inviting while also triggering within me a sense of inadequacy and otherness. In those homes, as in this one, I'd been amazed by their pantries and kitchens, filled with neatly organized, seemingly endless supplies of anything you might ever want to eat. There, I perfected the art of eating more than my fair share—often bingeing when I could find ways to be alone with their bountiful rations—and hiding the footprints of my transgressions, careful not to leave obvious clues of my private torment.

In Shonda's home that night, most of the cast sat on her large sectional, draped across cushions and wrapped in pastel-shaded pashminas, nibbling on snacks, and delighting in one another's company.

I sat on a stool on the far end of the room, at the corner of her enormous kitchen island, hiding behind a large tray of my own personal crudites. Stuffing my face nervously, I watched the cast watch the episode, watched them watch me. I was too anxious to watch my work up on the TV screen, and too terrified to share the experience with the group.

Back then I had a hard time watching myself. I was still struggling with my own image in the mirror—seeing myself on-screen was exponentially more difficult. Because premieres are a cause for celebration, sometimes I would cave to pressure from colleagues and sit through a screening. But if I could leave without watching the whole thing I almost always did, choosing instead to find somewhere to hide (and often eat) until the film was over.

But this was television—I couldn't hide until the end of the movie because the movie kept unfolding, week after week, episode upon episode.

Scandal broke my embargo on watching myself. Watch parties became a tradition for our *Scandal* family. Part of the reason we had these regular gatherings was because of our commitment to live tweeting. The speed at which we responded in real time to the audience made it feel almost impossible to tweet while the show was actually airing. We had to watch it beforehand to get a head start on drafting some of our posts.

While we were still filming the first handful of episodes, I hosted one of those initial watch parties in a basement screening room of an apartment building where I was living in the Mid-Wilshire section of Los Angeles, above a Five Guys. Shonda had given me a DVD of the episode. When I opened the DVD player, I found that someone had left a disc of season one of *Friends* inside.

"My God, you guys!" I said, holding up the DVD to show to my castmates. "This has to be a sign."

Even at this point, so early in the life of *Scandal,* we had proven ourselves to be the kind of cast that met on the weekends to rehearse, came to set to show support for one another even when we weren't on the call sheet, and constantly found ways to encourage each other, both on and off camera. Darby Stanchfield, who was the last actor to be cast in our pilot, wrote me a notecard on our very first day of working together filled with the kind of loving-kindness, generosity, gratitude, and support that is normally conveyed between lifelong friends. Luckily for me, that's what we eventually became. From the very beginning we were all one another's greatest fans. The relationships among the cast members on *Friends* were legendary—the friendships they'd created were as inspiring as the success of the show itself. I wanted that for us; we all did. So, as I loaded our episode of *Scandal* into the DVD player, I took extra care to turn the *Friends* DVD upside down so that it wouldn't get scratched.

While our friendships were seeded during our sixteen-hour workdays, five days a week, ten months a year, for seven years, it was in these moments when we came together on the weekends—with our spouses and our children and our dogs, having potluck dinners and sharing our lives and homes with one another—that I started to have a deeper understanding of what it felt like to find intimacy, safety, community, and belonging—a found family—all in one space.

~~~

After we made the pilot of *Scandal*, the network picked us up for a paltry six episodes. At the time, the standard episode order—for a show like *Grey's Anatomy*, for example—was twenty-two per year. Given the reality of having a Black female actor in the lead, the network's decision had undertones of risk aversion—having a Black woman helm a primetime television show was a gamble in their eyes. Executives considered it an enormous financial risk. They were unconvinced that audiences would tune in. Six episodes would allow them the chance to trial a hero that looked like me. But six episodes also meant that as creatives—the writers, the actors, the directors, the department heads—we had an opportunity to take our own risks, make bold choices, and break new ground.

Having only six episodes turned out to be integral to developing the intensity and rhythm of the show, because Shonda decided to pack those six episodes with ferocious plots and mind-bending twists. Once the show was established, the writers would work to maintain that tone and momentum for the next seven seasons—that adrenaline was part of the show's original DNA.

It's also what made live tweeting such an exhilarating part of the *Scandal* experience. Twitter helped to create an environment of must-watch event television at a time when DVR was becoming king and streaming was on the rise. When it was announced that *Scandal* would air as a mid-season replacement for a canceled show, it meant that we would debut during the spring, without the fanfare of an entire fall lineup that could have helped drive viewers to our initial season.

Allison Peters, a fellow Spence girl from the Bronx who had become a close friend and who was at the vanguard of the rise of social media, had encouraged me to open a Twitter account months before filming the pilot of *Scandal*. By the time we were airing, we both knew that a strong social media presence would help to support and uplift this "risky experiment" in television history. Allison suggested that what would work best would be for the entire cast to tweet while the show was airing. So, in Olivia Pope fashion, rather than being perceived as a bossy number one, I reached out to our boss, Shonda, who was also an early adopter of Twitter and who had experienced the excitement that had grown in online communities around *Grey's Anatomy* fan fiction. I asked Shonda to ask the cast to join Twitter and live tweet the shows. I also reached out to friends I had made through years of working in the entertainment business and was grateful for supportive posts from people like John Legend, Common, and Missy Elliott.

The genuine excitement on Twitter from our cast and crew toward one another, and from audiences toward the show, led to a grassroots movement of support. Fans called themselves

#Gladiators after the way an employee of Olivia Pope & Associates (Harrison, played by Columbus Short) refers to himself in the first scene of the pilot. And the ABC network had a new army of viewers that it couldn't ignore.

When we were granted an additional six episodes, and then a second season, we were ecstatic—we were not yet a hit, we were "on the bubble," as they say, but we were happy there *was* a season two; we were happy to be working, and working with one another.

As season two progressed, the growing social media frenzy surrounding the show expanded as our plots thickened and the show launched in territories all over the world. At the same time I was now the lead actress in a new Tarantino film—which is always a huge international event. Suddenly, this gamble of a show that executives thought might be too niche even for American audiences was being headlined by an international movie star and was becoming a global hit.

◇

It was the one-two punch of *Scandal* and *Django* that turned my life upside down.

For a girl who'd decided she wanted to be an actor even though she didn't want to be famous, this was an overwhelming time. I knew how lucky I was, I knew I was in rarefied air—living a life filled with dreams I didn't even know I had—but I was also terrified.

I imagine it's what surfing feels like in rough waters. Blessed with the opportunities and responsibilities that presented themselves because of *Scandal* and *Django,* I was no longer just an actor but also an advocate, a team leader, a cheerleader, an ambassador, a changemaker, a role model. Every day, I would get out of bed and head to set, and it felt like swimming out into a body of water that I could not control. I knew my job was to get on top of the waves and ride them, but I was in the storm that comes with rising fame. Rehearsed as I was in the performance of perfection, I tried to keep my struggles mostly private, below the surface of the waves. The recovery happened underwater—back on the board, I tried to make it look flawless.

Nevertheless, I was feeling lost. There was Olivia Pope—I spent most hours of the day thinking about who she was and what she wanted. How she walked; what she wore; what she said. There was "Kerry Washington," who had become an avatar for progress and inclusion and fashion and fame—she, too, had a calculated appearance and way of being. And then there was me, behind the scenes, the longshoreman at the end of the dock, in the middle of a nor'easter with my head down, working through the night. In some ways, my worldview became very small, and my circle of trust shrank.

I felt a distance growing between my friends outside of work and me. Trust requires consistency, and outside of work, I was at best inconsistent. Even now, I find it easier to maintain relationships with those who are most forgiving and allow me to disappear into the work. Back then, I was becoming closer to my fellow cast members and crew on *Scandal* because we were all on a rocket ship together. *Scandal* had become a cultural phenomenon and a pop culture reference. We had takeovers on talk shows. World leaders were referencing the show. There was a *Scandal* clothing line. I hosted *Saturday Night Live* and was on the cover of *Vanity Fair*. It's hard to explain what it felt like to be on that rocket ship, but for those of us on the ride, we clung to one another, made sense of it together, and built the kind of intimacy that genuinely redefined what friendships looked like for me and taught me how to be in deep connection.

Before *Scandal*, I was really good at walking onto a film set and becoming best friends with people for three months, then cutting ties and never seeing them again. On a film set, there is a kind of immediate closeness created, but because you know it's short-term, it can lack authentic intimacy or real vulnerability—you tend not to show the messiest parts of you. It was a familiar dynamic. I maintained a presentation of self for about one hundred days or so until the movies wrapped, and then I would move on.

But on *Scandal*, I started to drop the mask not only because the hours were long, over an extended period of time, but also because we knew we were part of something historic. We were committed to the show and to one another, and that rapid-fire intimacy didn't disappear—it lasted for seven years. Through the course of it I learned how to maintain and nurture authentic closeness and vulnerability over the long haul, through weddings and divorces and illness and births and good times and bad times and everything in between. I had come to understand, accept, and even embrace the limitations of intimacy with my parents. We had found an ease and fluidity with the veils and masks we donned. But with my *Scandal* family, the long hours and the creative commitment and the rare air of fame led to unguarded honesty and unbridled connection.

The relationships that Olivia Pope had with her associates, as well as those she had at the fictional White House, were intensely intimate, forged under high-stakes situations. She had a heroic commitment to the people in her life and used her talents for fixing in service of her friendships as much as for the clients who walked through the door.

That kind of intimacy didn't come naturally for me. But playing Olivia Pope helped.

She also helped me to lead. Being number one on the call sheet required an intense work ethic, stamina, and resilience. Part of why I was able to be number one was because I was playing a talented leader who stared down challenges and navigated situations that paralyzed other people. "It's my name on that door," I said week after week, and I thought, *It's my face on that poster, my name at the top of the credits.* Playing her on-screen helped me to step into an Olivia Pope version of myself, helped me find my own sense of capability and power.

Olivia Pope helped me to become a fixer and a leader in my real life.

~~~

Nnamdi and I got married in June 2013, in a relatively small ceremony in Sun Valley, Idaho, at the home of our friends Beth and Ron Dozoretz. For months I had been wearing my engagement ring secretly pinned inside my clothing for fear that if people knew we were engaged, it would be impossible to have a wedding away from public spectacle. All the planning happened in code. Our wedding planner was under strict confidentiality. We referred to the event as a family reunion to all our vendors, and verbal invitations went out just prior. Jason Wu, an old friend who had designed Michelle Obama's inaugural gown, agreed to design my dress, but, wanting to keep our secret even from his own team, he referred to the gown as "the dress I'm designing for the Moroccan premiere of *Scandal*."

As Nnamdi and I planned our wedding, we were aware that this singular day was not just a party but an opportunity to establish the culture of our marriage and our lives together. We wanted the details of the day to reflect where we came from, who we were, and the future we hoped to build together. My cousin Austin played the music that accompanied me down the aisle; Nnamdi's cousin Chike DJ'ed the reception; his sister Chisara officiated. From the Jamaican black cake to the second entrance we made, dressed in traditional Nigerian regalia (my Nigerian gown was designed and made by Nnamdi's younger sister, Udo), every aspect came from the shared truth of us. We were carving out our own rituals, some more traditional than others.

For years, I'd felt that the tradition of a bride being handed from her father to her husband—a formality that designated women as property in a household—was insulting. I knew that my dad would want to play an important role in the ceremony, but I did not feel that the gesture of being given from one man to another reflected the reality of the relationships between my dad and me, Nnamdi and me, or Nnamdi and my dad. I'd heard stories of women asking two or three parents or another trusted figure to walk them down the aisle, but none of that felt right for me. There was a loneliness that I felt in my family that wasn't entirely connected to my being an only child, a sense that when floating in the complexity of life's most intimate challenges, I was on my own.

I shared with my mother my intention to walk down the aisle by myself, to greet my husband at the altar as an independent woman making the choice to partner for life.

"Your father will be devastated," she said, leaving her own feelings unspoken.

I knew she was right. For the next few weeks, I wrestled with what to do. I didn't want my wedding ceremony to belong to my dad, to be carved in the image of his desires. But I also didn't want to embarrass him or reject him or make him feel less important on a day that was so deeply and divinely meaningful to me.

The day before the wedding, I went to see Beth and Ron's front yard, which was being transformed into a wedding venue. I noticed there were two thresholds I was to cross before reaching the altar, and a solution occurred to me, a compromise. So, on the day of the wedding, when I first appeared at the front door of the Dororetz home, I stood arm in arm with my dad, and we walked joyously toward our friends and family. But when we reached the rows of chairs encircling the outdoor altar, our journey together stopped. My dad walked ahead of me to greet Nnamdi and shake his hand while I waited. And then, once my dad sat down, I walked on my own through our small crowd of loved ones who had gathered in our honor, to where my future husband was standing with his brother, Chijoke.

I was my dad's daughter; Earl's kid; nothing was ever going to change that. But this new life, this new chapter, was being authored by me.

~~~

Usually, when I think about the story of where my family begins, I think of my mother's once upon a time. She and her siblings had grown up on Simpson Street in the South Bronx, and my cousins and I grew up hearing about the various mishaps and adventures that happened there. That street was their world. So, when I founded my production company in 2016—with the commitment to tell stories that center marginalized protagonists—Simpson Street was the name that I chose.

I didn't share this idea with my mom until she and two of her sisters were sitting beside me at the premiere of Simpson Street's first film, *Confirmation*. During the opening credits, the screen read, PRODUCED BY SIMPSON STREET, and I heard the three of them gasp.

Confirmation is a feature film I produced for HBO about the Anita Hill-Clarence Thomas hearings. Although I was fourteen when they happened, one of the reasons why the hearings stood out in my memory was that they were one of the few times my parents disagreed about politics. My dad now calls himself a feminist and admits his views have changed, but at the time he could not help but feel aligned with Thomas and felt compassion for the ways in which his reputation as a successful Black man was being tarnished on the national stage.

By contrast, my mother believed Anita Hill.

Having watched a recent documentary about the hearings, I knew there was a film to be made that could explore the intimate moments that the documentary wasn't privy to, and I thought it was important to share this legacy with new audiences. But when I went after the adaptation rights to the documentary, I found out another team of producers was also in pursuit, led by Susannah Grant and Michael London. I'd never produced before, but this, to me, felt like a story that should be presented and told by a Black woman. I reached out to Susannah and Michael and suggested that we make the film together—this way, I could offer my perspective and insight as both a storyteller and as a woman of color, and they, in turn, could teach me about producing.

We shot *Confirmation* on location in Atlanta in the summer between seasons three and four of *Scandal,* and I played Anita. Although the film is an exploration of many of the private moments surrounding this political story, as we developed the script, it became clear that recreating the hearings themselves would be vital.

Anita's testimony took place over the course of eight hours. Even after we'd distilled it for dramatic purposes, there were still a lot of words to memorize and behaviors to learn to adequately portray the story. My approach to learning the testimony was guided by the work of one of my greatest acting heroes, Anna Deavere Smith. I'd been inspired by her work since first seeing *Twilight: Los Angeles, 1992* on Broadway when I was in high school, and I was excited to borrow from her toolbox.

Anna works as a cultural anthropologist, recording interviews and then using those recordings as her source material. She memorizes her subjects' words but places equal significance on learning to mirror their breathing, their tonality, their rhythm, and their general physicality—it's as though she's bringing journalism to life. In each of her dramatic works, Anna transforms into various characters and creates poetic and moving performances by embodying the very essence of real people and speaking their words exactly as they said them.

Knowing how captivated viewers were by Anita Hill's actual testimony, I felt that Smith's approach would best allow me to honor the reality of the hearings. So, I watched Anita's testimony like a hawk, over and over, again and again. I looked for tenor and vocal placement and her breath patterns. I memorized not just the words but the posture, and the pauses, and the silences.

There were ways that I identified with Anita Hill. But my understanding of character—the process of developing a character—leaned heavily on understanding the outside expression of a character's interior life. Character, in acting terms, is often defined by *how* a person does things. Everyone engages in behavior: sleeping, walking, talking; and everyone has feelings: joy, sadness, fear, excitement. How we do those things, and how we express those feelings, helps define a character. How life is expressed uniquely by an individual is part of what makes us who we are. So, Anna Deavere Smith's approach was an exciting road map, guiding me away from myself and toward Anita Hill.

And unsurprisingly this process did unlock the character for me. After filming, I got one of the best compliments I've ever received as an actor when Anita Hill pulled me aside and said, "Kerry—I didn't know I had a walk!"

I laughed.

"No, really," she said, "I wasn't aware that I walked that way, but when I saw it, I knew it was me."

While this approach to character development—often described as an outside-in approach—was tremendously effective, there were moments of filming that required me to use entirely different acting tools. There are certain times when the embodiment of thoughts and feelings requires a more inside-out approach. If I know that a character is frustrated or afraid—two emotions that Anita Hill experienced at various moments throughout the hearings—in order to tap into those emotions I may ask the question, *What do I, Kerry, know about this feeling? How can I relate to this moment?* When I land on an answer, sometimes I'll try to engage in a "replacement exercise," where I imagine myself in a situation from my own life that triggers the feelings in me that are required for the scene, rather than imagining myself in the circumstances of the scene as written.

While we were filming the hearings, I sat in a replica of that famous turquoise dress, across the Senate floor from a long dais of actors playing politicians. When I first entered the room, I felt the flash of cameras that had been handed to background actors by the props department. As they had on the actual day, photographers clamored to capture Anita Hill's expression. As I sat at the table, it was impossible not to feel intimidated. The actors playing politicians sat about ten feet above me, each of them portraying a white man of a certain age, many of them with southern accents. The tension in the room was palpable. As an actor, it's exciting when an environment on set can so powerfully evoke the given circumstances and emotions of the scene — it is inspiring and helps to bring authenticity to what's captured on-screen. But as we were working toward suspending our audience's disbelief, I also had to suspend mine: because as powerless as I might have felt in that moment, in reality, each of those men was, in fact, working for me.

One of the elements of Anita Hill's life that I thought I could relate to most was the loss of privacy that was forced upon her. At the time there was a fever pitch surrounding *Scandal*. *TMZ* had obtained our marriage certificate while Nnamdi and I were honeymooning in Tanzania. When the marriage papers wound up online, I could feel the loss of control of my ability to protect my personal life. That situation intensified exponentially when news of my pregnancy leaked five months later while I was in New York hosting *SNL*. If there's one thing that paparazzi love to capture, it's the evolving pregnant body of a famous woman. From the moment that the press became aware (a leak that came from someone in the *Scandal* cast or crew), I was hounded by photographers — on set, in the street, on the freeway (I had to learn how to lose them on the highway so that they wouldn't follow me home and find out where we lived).

When Isabelle was eight weeks old, Nnamdi and I went to visit a home we had purchased in the Hollywood Hills that had just completed renovations. The next morning, long-lens photographs of us standing in our backyard holding her appeared online. After consulting with contractors, we realized there was no adequate way to block all views from the surrounding canyon and so, without ever moving in, we put that house on the market and began to search for a new home.

By the time Isabelle was a toddler, we had crafted a world full of tactics that helped us protect our children's privacy. We developed nicknames for the kids that were different from what appeared on their birth certificates because we knew there were paparazzi at parks looking for them (their birth certificates had gotten leaked, too). We had had security on the floor of the hospital both times I gave birth, and they helped us leave in the middle of the night through secret exits. For many years my kids thought that hotel lobbies looked like restaurant kitchens because we always entered through back doors and service elevators.

We felt this was something we had to do to protect our children, but I often felt trapped in this life of secrecy. I am not complaining about this—I knew this was the darker side of a wonderful privilege bestowed upon my family—but getting caught in a public whirlwind left me feeling hounded, exposed, vulnerable, and overly scrutinized. Anita Hill's loss of anonymity was born out of her choice to come forward for the greater democracy. Mine was born of a much less heroic choice, but with similar results. As a producer and an actor there was so much of myself that I was bringing to this story: my professional experience as a woman; my identity as a Black person; the pressures of being a daughter of whom so much is expected; watching my mother navigate academia; and now, my understanding of the cost of public notoriety. I felt these were the themes that the project would allow me to explore. And it did—but there was something else.

Toward the end of my shooting schedule, we came to the moment in the film when Anita's integrity is being questioned because she had not filed a report of harassment sooner. Her truth was in doubt because she had chosen to remain on good terms with Clarence Thomas through the years. It's hours into the hearing, but Anita has maintained her composure and grace. After trying to explain her motives and justify her behavior, Anita's response is one of her most vulnerable moments of the day.

"I know that it can happen," she says, "because it happened to me."

When I did the actor's homework of asking what I could offer of myself to make those words ring true, I realized that I, too, had a history of sexual trauma that had remained a secret for far too long, and that I, too, had chosen not to report it.

As I sat on set, I imagined that, instead of addressing a table of all-white older male senators, I was speaking to my mother and to neighbors and friends who knew the frozen boy, the boy who had betrayed me, night after night.

I clearly was not Anita Hill. I had not been through what she had been through, and our histories of trauma should not, cannot, be compared. But like her, I had minimized my abuser's transgressions, kept them a secret to protect him, knowing also that the world might not believe me or would diminish the importance of what I'd experienced. On set that day, I used Anita Hill's words and her story to explain and defend my truth about what had happened to me, and why I had chosen to remain silent for so long.

I revealed my emotional truth to embody and honor hers. Offering up of some part of myself, in service of Anita Hill's truth, allowed me catharsis and healing. And for that I will be forever grateful.

~~~

This period of acting on *Confirmation*, and on *Scandal* the year before, marked a shift in my dominant approach to developing character and scene study. Early on, my approach to performance was guided by my desire to experience some sense of clear identity and emotional truth. Olivia Pope had proven to be an excellent opportunity for me to try to discover a version of myself that was more powerful, assertive, elegant, emotionally expressive. Olivia Pope was a true compassionate leader, too, and she taught me to be that both on and off set.

Being given the responsibility of playing Olivia made me move through the world in entirely new ways. Like Anita Hill, Olivia's walk was not my walk, but I found it by asking the question, *If I had the courage and confidence to be Olivia Pope,*

how might I move through the world? She, like so many characters before her, gave me something to reach for in order to
honestly and adequately portray her. Even with food and exercise, having to be her clarified my choices — I worked out and
ate in ways that would sustain Olivia Pope's physicality. And
in that way, the responsibility of being her saved me from the
darkest corners of myself.

But during the course of the show, I got pregnant twice.
For both pregnancies, Shonda was one of the first people to
know — before my own mother. The first time, I asked Shonda
if we could make Olivia pregnant. She was adamantly against
it. I didn't understand why at the time, but in hindsight, having
become a mother and subsequently played mothers, like Mia
in *Little Fires Everywhere,* and Kendra in *American Son*, I have
come to understand the inherent vulnerability of motherhood,
and Black motherhood in particular — the fear and anxiety
that develops when faced with the powerlessness of parenting
a Black child who must navigate and attempt to survive the
racism that is ingrained in our culture and institutions. This
vulnerability was not compatible with the parameters of Olivia
Pope's character.

When I got pregnant, I realized that my body was no
longer entirely my own. I was going to have to make choices
around food and exercise that were not in alignment with
Olivia Pope's reality. And I was going to change physically
in ways that seemed to be in direct opposition to the carefully crafted physique I had built for her. It became a crisis for
me. I use my physicality as an important tool in discovering

a character and what they're going through, but my body was going off into a crazy sci-fi adventure, whereas Olivia's was not. How could I be Olivia Pope if we weren't going to share a body? If I couldn't embody her, how could I play her? I knew that millions of people had grown accustomed to how Olivia looked and moved, but I worried that as my belly grew, I wouldn't be able to walk up and down the hallways of the White House the way Olivia Pope did.

But I also didn't want to feel like I was hiding. In the early seasons my journey playing Olivia Pope involved learning to be on the posters, to be number one on the call sheet, to live a very visible life.... It was important to stand behind my work, and I was determined to allow myself to be seen as the center of this groundbreaking show. And Olivia's storylines had been about facing the truth and not hiding from it; hiding a pregnant body was counterintuitive to who she was. In the pilot episode of the series, we learn that Olivia wants to end her relationship with the president because she loathes secrets. It's also what she says to her clients: "I have one rule: Do not lie. If you lie, all bets are off."

Terrified that I was going to betray the character and the show and our millions of viewers, and faced with this new acting challenge, I reached out to an acting coach I'd never worked with before, Kim Gillingham.

When I arrived at Kim's loft in Silver Lake in Los Angeles and explained my predicament, one of her first questions was, "If you can't give your body to Olivia as you have before, what else can you give?"

If I had to hide my belly behind boxes and coats and tables, could I reveal more of my heart instead? I'd always been enthusiastically willing to devote my body to a character because my body had never felt like my own anyway. Decades of abandoning and abusing myself to avoid feelings made my body an open vessel to be utilized at the disposal of my craft. Once I got pregnant, the reality of being a person who was growing a new human inside her necessitated a deeper relationship with my true self.

Kim was giving me permission to devote my body to the sacred, creative endeavor of pregnancy while learning new ways to cultivate and conjure the magic of acting. I was invited to devote my inner life to the character. Kim's belief is that characters and their circumstances come to actors because there is a need in the actor's subconscious to explore or express specific ideas that are engendered by the work. This for me was a paradigm shift—perhaps there were ways that I could more deeply understand Olivia by understanding myself, as opposed to the other way around? As with the testimony scene in *Confirmation* filmed years later, I began to understand that in bringing myself to the character rather than escaping myself to find her, together we were able to express a mutual, shared truth, not just an imaginary one outlined in the pages of a script.

Suddenly, my identity, my history, my feelings, my life as Kerry mattered in a new way.

~⁓~

With Kim's coaching, and a new pathway toward maintaining my work as Olivia Pope, I was freed to embrace this new chapter in my life as Kerry Washington. I couldn't bring my pregnancy to the role, but I could bring it to work.

Shondaland, as benevolently ruled by Shonda Rhimes, is a family-friendly place. I knew this because early in our first season I had gone to our line producer, Merri Howard, and confided in her that I had a secret boyfriend who played in the NFL in Philadelphia. I asked Merri if there was any way to manipulate my schedule to allow for my days off — of which I only had maybe one every other episode — to fall on a Monday, as that was Nnamdi's only day off. About once every two weeks, Merri made it possible for me to fly to Philadelphia and be there for Nnamdi when he returned home from his Sunday game.

Even in the face of our grueling production schedule, Merri — herself a devoted wife and mother — understood and did everything she could to support the dream I was working toward in my personal life: to marry Nnamdi, to be a bonus mom for his beautiful daughter, Anaiya, and, God willing, to bring some additional children into the fold.

The day I told Shonda I was pregnant, she literally jumped for joy in my trailer. Any woman who's had to tell a boss she's pregnant knows that this is an uncommon response from a chief executive.

On the contrary, Shonda threw me a baby shower, which at that point in my life was the most extravagant party I'd ever attended. My mother-in-law, Lilian, said grace and blessed the event, and my mother offered me, and all the moms in the room, some heartfelt wisdom about the journey of motherhood that lay ahead. I sat at a table surrounded by some of the most important women in my life—my mother and mother-in-law; Chisara and Udo; and three of my biggest role models: Jane Fonda, Diahann Carroll, and Cicely Tyson.

Once Isabelle was born, Shonda, Viola Davis, and I built a playroom at Sunset Gower Studios for our children to share. I brought Isabelle to work, where she'd nurse and take naps in my trailer over the course of my sixteen-hour filming days. We even created a code word for breastfeeding because the assistant directing (AD) department felt they should be discreet about it and not reference my breasts over the walkie-talkies. "Number one is hummingbird," they'd say. For my daughter's first Christmas, the AD department gave me a hummingbird ornament that we still hang on our tree every year.

～～

Scandal table reads were legendary.

Often the reads were cold (meaning we hadn't seen the script ahead of time), but because we operated like an intimate theater company, there was no holding back. Scenes in TV shows are filmed out of order, and we knew the table read was our only opportunity to rehearse the episode—our one-act play of the week—as a cohesive narrative, so we threw ourselves into the process with a deep emotional commitment.

Shonda loves theater actors. Linda Lowy, who casts all of Shonda's shows, was moving offices one day, and her husband, Jeff Perry—the cofounder of Chicago's legendary Steppenwolf Theatre Company—was helping her move. Shonda commented that it was unfortunate that such a great actor was unable to find a gig and was now forced to work for a moving company. "No, that's my husband!" Linda said, and Shonda cast him immediately on *Grey's Anatomy*, and eventually as Cyrus Beene on *Scandal*.

When reading our episodes, occasionally I had the feeling that my character was going through situations that somehow mirrored my own. This was not unique to me or to *Scandal*—actors in long-running TV shows often talk about a kind of feedback loop that gets established. Week after week actors bring life to words on the page; the writers, sitting in an edit bay or at Video Village (the area on set designated for writers and producers to watch scenes as they are filmed in real time), witness not only the actors' interpretation of the script but also who that actor is between takes. Tiny details begin to pop up in scripts inspired by what the writers see. Sometimes the process is more obvious. At the start of our second season, when Shonda asked me if I had any special skills that she didn't know about, I shared with her that I loved the water, that I was a strong swimmer, that *Splash* was my favorite movie as a child, and that I was on the swim team at Spence. Later that season, Shonda made Olivia Pope a swimmer. She'd sometimes swim to sort through her thoughts when wrestling with a difficult issue. To help it make sense for audiences, Tony Goldwyn's character explains, "Olivia Pope was on the swim team in high school."

We filmed all our pool scenes at the Los Angeles Athletic Club in downtown LA. On our first day of filming underwater,

I was introduced to an entirely new camera crew, as the scenes required operators who were certified to dive and had specialized knowledge of waterproof equipment.

"Listen," the operator said to me, "the scene is written for your character to swim fast, so the director has asked me to do whatever I can to make that believable. I have some thoughts about how to shoot this to get that idea across, but just do whatever you can to keep up with me."

This'll be fun, I thought.

When I was a kid, we played a game at Jamie Towers called All Sharks Under. I was the first girl in the neighborhood ever allowed to play. Whoever was "it" would sit on their own, on one side of the pool, and call out "All sharks under!" to the crowd of kids waiting on the other side. Each "shark" from the crowd would then dive in with the goal of making it across the pool without coming up for air. Whoever was "it" would attempt to catch the sharks and force them to the surface. If you failed to make it across — if you were caught and dragged to the top and forced to breathe — you, too, became part of the "it" team. The goal of the game was to be the last shark left in the pool. To make it across you had to know the weaknesses of the other sharks, be willing to forge alliances, be able to hold your breath for long periods of time, and above all, you had to be fast.

As the crew readied themselves for "action," I clung to the edge like it was the Jamie Towers pool all those years ago. Our director shouted "Action!" but what I heard was "All sharks under!"

I swam across the pool as if I were defending my neighbor-hood nickname, Fish. The camera operator had no choice but to follow my wake. When I got to the other end of the pool, he lifted his scuba mask and laughed.

"OK," he said, "let's try this again. Maybe you could slow down a little...?"

~~~

Sometimes, with the writers' help, we brought ourselves to the characters; and sometimes, in the pursuit of the character's truth, the writers helped us to find our own.

Katie Lowes, who played Quinn Perkins, got married one year before me, but maybe because she is younger, or maybe because she didn't grow up with an acute awareness of how difficult she'd been to conceive, she hadn't rushed into becoming a mom. I had embraced the role of bonus mom as soon as I knew that Nnamdi was the man I wanted to spend the rest of my life with. And once we were married, I jumped into thoughts of having more children right away. Katie and her husband, Adam, hadn't made that leap yet. And it was a topic we talked about often between takes.

Late in season six, the writers created a beautiful scene in which Olivia Pope, having decided to leave her private firm to work at the White House, appoints Quinn Perkins as the new head of the crisis management office, changing OPA—Olivia Pope & Associates—to QPA, Quinn Perkins & Associates.

When Quinn insists that she's not sure she's ready to run the firm, Olivia Pope disagrees. I knew in preparing for the scene that there was a truth between Katie and me that mirrored Olivia's truth with Quinn's. I saw the dialogue scene as an opportunity to tell Katie that, like Quinn, she was ready. The words on the page were about her running Pope & Associates, but we both knew that the subtext and the emotions that I was expressing to her were about her capacity to step into the leadership of her family and take the leap into motherhood. We were both moved to tears that day; both Quinn's truth and Katie's were undeniable. They were ready.

Today, Katie and Adam have two children, and she runs a wildly successful podcast on Shondaland's platform about parenting.

~~~

In the history of *Scandal*, we had one guest star I called home to tell my parents about.

Joe Morton is an absolute supernova, and a hero of mine. *The Brother from Another Planet* was the first independent film I truly loved, and his performance in it expanded my understanding of what stories about Black people could look like.

When Joe first appeared on *Scandal*, his role was cryptic. His character was a kind of mystery puppet master, and although I desperately wanted to act with him, week after week I was denied the opportunity.

"Boy, I really hope we get the chance to work together one day," I said at the end of a table read as we neared the end of the season.

He looked at me and smiled.

In the final episode of the season—an episode that none of the actors had seen before the table read—Olivia Pope is leaving her apartment to go running and winds up being attacked by paparazzi. When a car pulls up to rescue her, Olivia climbs inside and stares incredulously at the man sitting across from her. The final line of the episode—and the season—was a question. Olivia Pope looks at the character of Rowan, played by Joe Morton, and, trying to make sense of the shocking revelation of his presence, says, "Dad?"

At the table read the room erupted in shock, all except my TV dad. Joe had known all along that he was playing my father.

❧

When I was eleven, my dad and I were swimming in the lake at our house upstate. I remember feeling lucky to be in that place with that man, doing something we both loved to do. We were laughing, treading water, slowly gliding toward the center of the lake, casually enjoying our time.

At one point, my dad looked at me with a glimmer in his eye and smiled.

"What?" I said.

He looked across the lake to our dock, then back across to the other side, then back to our dock.

"What do you think?" he said.

We'd never swum across the lake before. By my estimates, we were closer to our own dock than the other side, but the other side was an adventure within reach; it just meant traversing unknown depths in the center.

I was nervous, but I was with my dad, and in his eyes, I could do anything. I knew it would be easier and less scary to go back to our own dock, but his deep belief in the possibility of triumph made it impossible not to give it a shot. Wanting to make him proud, I pushed myself to take the risk.

"Let's do it!" I said.

We hadn't told anyone we were going to swim all that way. No one was watching us; there was no one in a canoe beside us; no life vests were in reach. No one would be waiting for us to arrive on the other side, but the house whose dock we had in our sights was owned by friends of our family, Lou and Tony, and we knew they'd at least have a pair of towels for us when we arrived.

We angled our bodies toward their dock and smiled.

"Mom's going to kill us," I said. Then we laughed and started to swim.

As we made our way across, the journey felt longer than we'd anticipated, and in a moment of pause, we turned on our backs to float on the water and gaze at the scudding clouds. Eventually we flipped over, determined to meet the pace of the clouds, and continued on.

By the time we got to Lou and Tony's dock, they were waiting for us, towels in hand.

"Why didn't you call to warn us you were coming?" they joked as we pulled ourselves out of the water.

"Oh, we were just in the neighborhood," my dad said, catching his breath.

My dad taught me to believe that I could do anything—
that day, before, and always. We walked home laughing, barefoot and exhausted.

When we got home, my mother was scared and furious.

"Where have you *been*?" she said. "Whose *towels* are those?"

I proudly recounted our victory and saw both her delight
and disapproval. From that moment on, rules were established
in our extended family that no one was to swim across the lake
without an adult present, and you had to have double digits in
your age to even try.

There was no turning back. What had seemed impossible
just hours before was now the basis of a new family ritual. As
my mother scolded us, my dad and I smiled at each other and
silently enjoyed the truth that treasures could be found on the
other side of a trial. Between us there was only unmitigated joy,
and a new bond as wide as our beloved lake.

CHAPTER THIRTEEN

REVELATION

"Forty-three years ago, we were having a really hard time having a child..."

"Yes. OK," I said. This was not news to me.

"So, we used a surrogate."

What?

"No," my mother corrected herself, "I mean..." She fumbled. "We used sperm, we used sperm from another man."

Unaccustomed to seeing my mother struggle with either her words or her feelings, I tried to help her.

"Do you mean artificial insemination?"

She nodded yes and then looked at my dad, but he continued to stare down at the rug.

"From a sperm donor?" I asked.

He groaned with pain at the mere mention of this.

"Yes," she said, finally looking right at me.

A wave of heat rose in me. An urgency raced through my veins. Once again, I was a swimmer, hanging off the side of a pool, waiting to explode forward into the conversation. I looked at my parents *(do I still call them my parents?)* and opened my mouth to speak. But before I could say anything, I saw the heartache that they were swimming in, and my questions got trapped inside my concern for them.

"Wow," I said, forcing a hint of laughter, hoping to lighten their load. "Thank you for telling me. I know that must have been hard."

I was not—am not—my dad's biological daughter.

I am not, as I had been told, the genetic sum of the human beings who sat across from me. I am not who I had been told I was, from the very beginning of my existence. But somehow, the gift of finally knowing the truth outweighed the pain of what that truth was. In that moment, I was liberated by the revelation. They had never, I suddenly realized, been fully honest with me, not until that afternoon. They had entered into an illusory contract with each other to lie to everyone, including me, and themselves, about the truth of our biological ties and the reality of my origins. And now, here we were, forty-one years later, the original lie between us exposed, the truth laid bare.

My mother, perhaps knowing that there was no going back, continued to share: Her ob-gyn was a specialist in infertility—she had sought him out after her stillbirth, unaware that he was also at the cutting edge of experimental practices. He made a suggestion; it was all very secret.

"Do you know where the sperm came from?" I asked.

"No."

"Have you ever tried to find out?"

"No."

"Did you want to know?"

She shook her head.

"No. Our only asks were that he be healthy, and that he be Black."

I looked back at my dad, hunched over, spine still curled into the corner of the couch. He appeared to me like a trunk full of treasure that had sunk to the bottom of the ocean.

"He was Black," I said, starting to collect clues. "So that no one would know?"

"Yes," she said, calmly. I could hear the relief in her voice, the resolve. She was done hiding.

I smiled lovingly at my mother. I was so grateful to her for this gift of truth.

But looking again at my dad, I could tell he needed me. I got up and crossed the room to sit on the couch beside him. He groaned again. Something in him was dying. I put my hand on his leg.

"Hey," I said. "It's OK..."

"No, no, no—" He tried to cut me off, but I stopped him, emboldened by the wisdom of what I didn't know.

"Dad," I said, definitively. *Dad.* I knew what he needed to hear: "Nothing is going to change between us. This won't impact our love."

I thought about how, when I was pregnant the second time, I made a point to reassure my toddler about the arrival of her brother by explaining that my heart would not now be cut in half, but that my capacity for love would instead double. I promised her that there would be room in my heart, and on my lap, for all three of my children. Similarly, I didn't know if I would ever meet or know or love the mystery man who I had just learned was responsible for half of my biology, but I was immediately convinced and committed to the idea that whatever I felt for that man would not negate what I felt for the dad sitting beside me.

"How do you feel?" Dad deflected, trying to take the focus off his pain.

Excited, elated, alive, electric.

But I could read the room. My joy stood alone. They were still navigating the devastation of having to share a secret they thought they might take to their graves.

Unwilling to betray my truth, but willing to temper my excitement—because even I was surprised that my feelings were not more complicated, more tortured—I answered, "Curious..."

My mother smiled.

"I feel...curious," I repeated. I was finding myself.

I took a few deep breaths. No one spoke. And then reluctantly my dad said, "I can understand that."

"When were you going to tell me?" I asked them both.

"Never," he said. "There was nothing to tell."

I didn't push him on what he meant.

"My plan," my mother confided, "was to maybe write you a letter one day and leave it in a safe-deposit box for after we were gone." But she was nearing eighty and had survived cancer and had not yet written such a letter, so in my mind I questioned when that plan would have been executed.

"The crazy thing," I said to them both, still holding on to my dad's leg, "is that our whole lives we have loved one another under false pretenses. Starting today, you'll get to see that even though I know the truth, I still love you."

And then I turned to my dad and leaned into him.

"Now you'll get to feel what it's like to be loved unconditionally," I said.

~~~

A few months earlier, I was leaving a fancy luncheon celebrating women in the film and television industry at the Beverly Wilshire Hotel when I noticed Professor Henry Louis Gates Jr., affectionately known as "Skip," walking toward me. I was an enormous fan of his and of his PBS series *Finding Your Roots,* and for years we had talked about the possibility of me joining his roster of guests so that I, too, could find out about my ancestry and family ties. Until that moment, my schedule at *Scandal*—and the way that I had packed each hiatus with film- and baby-making—made it impossible to commit to a project like this, but as Professor Gates walked toward me, I got excited. We were waist-deep in the process of filming our final season, and with the public announcement of our decision to end the show, new opportunities and possibilities were presenting themselves. I knew that in the coming months I would finally be able to find the time to sit down with Professor Gates and learn more about myself.

Years before, when Isabelle was eight months old, Oprah Winfrey had invited Nnamdi and me to her home in Montecito for a weekend brunch where we could get to know each other more and celebrate our birthdays, hers being three days before mine. I remember sitting on the couch in the hallway of OPA, talking to Katie Lowes and Guillermo Diaz with nervous excitement about what I was going to wear (on the day, I wound up changing my mind at the last minute to better complement the outfit I had chosen for my infant). When we arrived at Oprah's estate and sat for lunch, she almost immediately launched into a series of intensely intimate, *Oprah Winfrey Show*–type questions: Why had we gotten married? What did marriage mean to us? How old was Anaiya? How had having a newborn changed our relationship?

And then a new line of questioning emerged. Toward the end of my second trimester, Nnamdi had made the decision to retire from an eleven-year career as a shutdown cornerback in the NFL. Before taking a bite of our second course, Oprah shared that for her, retirement—her decision to leave her groundbreaking talk show—had created a sea change in her life.

"Who are you now, Nnamdi?" she asked. "Who are you if you are no longer a football player?"

We were in our fourth season of *Scandal,* but I knew that this wild ride would not last forever. I had been in the business long enough to understand that while we were still close to the top, nothing lasts forever. As I sat and waited for my husband to answer Oprah's question, part of me pondered what a question like that would mean for me. The rise of *Scandal* had made both Kerry Washington and Olivia Pope household names, and my devotion to that character had shaped a great many of my choices and decisions. Being Olivia Pope had helped me step into being Kerry Washington: actress, advocate, activist, fashion and beauty personality, producer, wife, mother. Her fearlessness had propelled me forward into a life that was bigger and bolder than the one I had imagined for myself. I wondered, *When it was time to say goodbye to Olivia Pope, who would I be?*

Bumping into the professor that afternoon, and discussing the possibility of exploring who I am and where I come from, seemed like the perfect way to embrace what might be a rocky transition away from the emotional security and familiarity of being Olivia Pope. It was time to let go of this character who had first inspired me to reach for more greatness in myself to bring her to life, and who then gave me permission to reveal more of my truth from behind the mask of her existence. She was going to disappear from televisions, and from the narrative of my life. I had, in many ways, found myself in the years between when we shot the pilot for *Scandal* and now. But chatting with Skip, I knew that it was time to discover more about who I was apart from her. And he could help me do that.

~∼~

When I told my parents about my scheduled appearance on *Finding Your Roots,* they both seemed excited at first, enthusiastic about the process of discovery that might introduce us to more of ourselves and our ancestry. My mother offered to share the large amount of research she had already done on her family tree, but I explained to them that in addition to census reports and public records, *Finding Your Roots* would also use genealogy and examine our DNA.

Soon after that, my dad's panic attacks started.

I wondered if it had anything to do with his recent diagnosis of COPD. I thought that perhaps his increased difficulty breathing had been exacerbated by anxiety about uncovering some immoral, illegal, or unjust behavior of a long-lost relative. I insisted, "We have nothing to be afraid of. There's nothing that we will uncover that will tarnish who we are today."

But the panic attacks continued, and he was unable to sleep at night. So, I set a call for Professor Gates to speak privately with my parents to assuage their concerns.

Months later, Skip told me that during the call, my mother asked what I think she hoped sounded like a hypothetical question.

"If Kerry had been conceived in a way that was not biologically related to her father, would that kind of thing come up in a DNA test?"

Professor Gates said that yes, it would.

"And is that something we would have to share with her?" she asked.

Skip told me that while he did not tell my parents what to do on that call, he did share with them that during his many years of working on the show, he had seen these kinds of situations arise, and that it was always better for the family when they were able to process the truth together, while everyone was still alive. My parents told Skip that they still didn't think they wanted to appear on the show—especially now that DNA testing would be involved. Skip said that he understood and offered to put my parents on the phone with the resident geneticist from the show, CeCe Moore. She, too, confirmed that a DNA test would indeed reveal the truth, and that if my dad was not my biological father, that secret would indeed be revealed. CeCe encouraged them to be honest with me regardless of whether we were going to appear on the show or not.

When my parents told me that they'd spoken with Skip and CeCe, it was not shocking to learn that acquaintances and strangers knew more about me than I knew about myself. It felt sadly similar to what I'd been through with Worthbern, but now the secrets being kept from me were not only details about my parents' lives, they were fundamental truths about my own.

~~~

When I left the apartment that afternoon I went home, saw my children, asked them questions about their day at Candytopia, and scrolled through pictures of their adventures. I smiled at them and hugged them and held them, but the ground beneath me had shifted. The truth about me had been transformed and therefore, I realized, theirs had, too.

I sat looking in their eyes, knowing that their grandfather wasn't who they thought he was, that I wasn't, either, and that they weren't who they knew themselves to be. My inability to tell them trapped me in a legacy of withholding that I did not ask for and did not want. Suddenly, I, too, was keeping secrets from my children. I felt silenced and lost because I had been given a truth, but was unable to share it. I was unable to orient myself in the moment as if in a fog. I forced myself to stand and announced to everyone in the room that I was heading upstairs to change for dinner.

When I walked into my bedroom and closed the door behind me, I could hear Nnamdi moving around in the closet. When he finally appeared, the sight of him was like a buoy, a lifesaving beacon of belonging, a desert island after decades adrift.

He smiled at me, then sat with his back toward me on the edge of the bed to put his shoes on, and casually tossed two questions over his right shoulder.

"Everything good? What did your parents want to talk about?"

~~~

Later that evening, Nnamdi sat on the edge of our bed and held the phone on speaker. My mother was asking if we still wanted them to join us for dinner that night. I pulled the blinds to our bedroom, closing us off from the outside world. We looked at each other and silently agreed to not change our plans. Reservations for a local restaurant, Pace, had been set for six people: it would be my parents; my cousin John and his wife, Milly; and Nnamdi and me. Canceling the dinner would have been too much of a signal to my family, and most importantly to myself, that some life-shattering change had just unfolded. With John and Milly at the table, there would be ample justification to behave as though nothing had changed. I knew this would be a comfort for my parents' tremendous fear that the news they'd shared would cause an irreparable rupture. And while I didn't yet know what this new information meant for me, I knew that there was safety in playing Kerry Washington as I'd understood the role up until that point. My job that night was to be the gracious host, the perfect child, the good girl. The solution.

~~

Pace is a cozy neighborhood bistro cradled in the twists and turns of Laurel Canyon. The tables at Pace are covered in brown paper, and at the center of each sits a small tumbler filled with ragged crayons to keep hungry people distracted and occupied. Our server, knowing Nnamdi's usual predilection, asked him if he wanted to begin with dessert. He usually orders dessert as an appetizer because he doesn't want to run out of room for the things he loves most. As we waited for his apple crumble (a la mode) to arrive, laughing lovingly at his nonconformity, I noticed him scribbling across from me with one of the broken crayons. My cousin John, who sat to Nnamdi's left, was the visual artist of our family. After a childhood spent drawing comic books, and an adolescence spent tagging walls all over New York City with graffiti that was, to some, a crime of delinquency, but to many of my generation, high art, John graduated from the School of Visual Arts in New York City. He has woven art into his work, first as a graphic designer, and now as a community organizer and youth advocate.

I saw John do a double take at the space in front of Nnamdi and leaned forward to get a closer look at what my husband had been doodling. There, in front of him, lay an impeccably drawn tableau of street art, a hip-hop caricature of a young guy in a baseball cap, surrounded by urban buildings under a streetlamp.

I had no idea my husband, whom I'd known for over a decade, had an ounce of talent for drawing.

"Did you draw that?" John said, blown away by how good it was.

Nnamdi laughed and shrugged.

"Yeah," he said.

John looked at me and smiled.

"Not bad," John said.

But I was nonplussed—*had they played a trick on me? Had they switched seats when I wasn't looking?* I looked at the drawing, then I looked at Nnamdi, wondering what else I might learn today.

I was careful not to make too much of the absurdity, afraid that maybe I was projecting the revelation of the afternoon onto this much smaller surprise. But still the thoughts remained: *Is anyone at this table who I thought they were? My husband is suddenly a visual artist; my dad is suddenly unrelated to me; my mother is both my betrayer—complicit in the charade of my identity—and now, also the harbinger of truth.*

So, who the fuck am I?

~~~

I love all things Disney. I understand this may sound childish, or like the statement of a person too naïve to hold the complex realities of a company rooted in commercialism, consumerism, and consumption, and tainted with a history of racism and misogyny. But the truth is that the circumstances of my upbringing seeded in me an undeniable draw toward the magical escapism and curated fantasy of the happiest place on Earth. There has never been a time that a stroll down Main Street inside the Magic Kingdom has not filled me with a sense of ease and peace. I was well into my twenties before I was able to exit a Disney theme park without crying.

I don't have this relationship with other theme parks, or other entertainment companies. It is Disney's deep ethos of imagination that I feel connected to, the commitment to magical thinking and to the journeys of heroes and the possibilities of miracles and the belief that wishes really do come true. It's no coincidence that ABC, a subsidiary of Disney, was the company willing to take the "risk" to put Olivia Pope on TV, and my alignment with their aspirational ethos is part of why Simpson Street is still with the company today. It's Disney's ability to redefine reality that speaks to me—the exhaustive attention to tiny details and the larger "imagineering" of immersive experiences.

Even now, although there are no more tears when I visit a Disney park (though there are plenty when I'm watching a Pixar movie), I am still awed by the artful world-building and powerful storytelling and the company-wide ability to transport hearts and minds. It was the escape I was always looking for as a child. And it is the song of my dad's heart, the language of his love. Reality holds no sway over my dad's dreams and is no match for his storytelling prowess. My dad wished upon stars all the time and for many things: success, love, wealth, family. And when my mother became pregnant with me, I became an answer to his prayers. I was evidence of the divine, proof of the miraculous. I was their little princess, and our lives together a fairy tale. We were supposed to live happily ever after. Perhaps that's why the land of make-believe always feels like home to me.

The day after the revelation, we all went to Disneyland, on a trip that had been planned weeks earlier in anticipation of my cousins' visit. As we roamed the park, I felt a shift in the narrative—sitting in the apartment with my parents the day before, I had been offered the role of a lifetime. After decades spent working to unearth the truth of various characters, it was finally my turn. I had asked questions of my characters, but there had been a reason I had been unable to ask the questions of myself: "Who am I?" "What do I want?" "How do I feel?" I had not been given the assignment of playing my true self; the role my parents had required of me was the role that best supported *their* story. My parents' obfuscation of who I was had led to a family culture of veiled secrecy and the avoidance of intimate truths, and in that void, I had been left alone to make sense of the disconnection and isolation that haunted our home. Those were the dynamics that protected their narrative.

But now, truth in hand, for the first time, I was starting to understand my story.

I stared at my parents as they sat next to each other on the "it's a small world" ride and wondered how ready they were for the adventure that I felt called to embark on. No longer was I walking through the world like one of those old-school Disney princesses, stuck in a slumber, waiting to be rescued, or hidden in a tower away from the truth of who I really was. The secret was out; the spell had been broken. The tide was turning, and it was time for me to step into a story of my own.

~~~

I wanted to find out who my biological father was.

My whole life, I'd felt as though there were a puzzle of a painting hanging in our living room with one piece from another puzzle jammed into place as if it belonged. Every day we all walked by it, admiring the painting and ignoring that piece. When my parents told me the truth about how I'd been conceived, it was as though our family had finally said, "This is not actually a painting—it's a puzzle. And if you look closely, that isn't even the right piece."

Acknowledging the truth of us was a relief, but we were still left with an incomplete puzzle—it was more honest, but now it carried with it a void.

I wanted to locate that missing piece; I wondered if knowing my donor would pave the way toward knowing more of myself.

While my dad remained uncomfortable discussing the question of my paternity, my mother was now an open book. She was eager to share any information with me that she thought might be helpful. We talked about how they'd made the decision, and where, and when. She gave me the name of the doctor who had supervised the inseminations and the location of his office. And even though my mother had asked her physician to destroy her medical records, I began a quest to uncover the identity of my donor.

My mom told me her vivid memory of being in the doctor's office after he'd analyzed my dad's sample.

"You have two choices," the doctor had said, "adoption, or artificial insemination."

My dad has no memory of that conversation. When it's brought up, his face contorts, and he shakes his head and sometimes chuckles with exasperation as he resists the idea that his memory may be faulty. I can see the traffic jam of thoughts squirreling around in his brain as he tries to make sense of a story that is told about him but that he cannot make his own.

It's no surprise that my mother and I experienced a rapid acceleration of intimacy—the reality was that she had not told a soul; this was the greatest secret of her life. So, after they disclosed the news to me, in some ways I went from being her daughter to one of her closest girlfriends, because I was now witness to the most vulnerable parts of her.

To my dad, the sperm donation was merely a boost, an insurance policy, akin to taking vitamins. As was common at the time, with every insemination my mother received in the office, the doctor then prescribed that my mom and dad go home and have sex. Intercourse does indeed make the body more susceptible to conception after insemination, but it was more than that: the doctor was giving my parents the gift of plausible deniability. And without the invention of genetic testing, this "gift" was supposed to allow them to never have to reveal the complicated circumstances of how I came to be.

To my dad, there was never a question: I was his. Even the doctor had said that no one would ever be able to prove otherwise.

Understanding how uncomfortable my dad was, I tried to embark on the journey without forcing him to participate. I quickly discovered that my mother's ob-gyn had long since closed his practice. Through the help of some retired New York City police officers and a private investigator, I learned that the doctor had actually passed away, as had his receptionist.

I was sure if I could have talked to this doctor, he would have remembered who the donor was. His practice served a fancy Upper East Side clientele, and I imagine that in the mid-1970s, he could have counted on one hand the number of Black women who had walked into his office and agreed to what was then a still highly experimental approach to conception. I understood my parents' resistance to sharing this information with me when I was a child, but I'd been an adult for more than two decades. There had been so much time lost.

When I asked my mother why she didn't tell me sooner, she said that it had never felt like the right time. She insisted that it would have been inappropriate when I was a child and then admitted that she was too afraid to tell me when I was in college and in the depths of my depression and eating disorder.

I reminded her that there were a couple of decades unaccounted for in her reasoning, but she had no answer for those.

While both my parents spent forty years keeping the truth from me, my dad seemed to do it out of a genuine psychological disconnect, an absolute denial of the truth of himself and of me—a denial required to maintain his identity, and mine. Whereas my mother made the daily choice to know the truth but betray reality and withhold it from me, that same truth simply did not exist for my dad.

At times I find myself angrier with my mother because in her decision to withhold the truth from me, she withheld herself from me. She was afraid that if we got too close, she might be tempted to reveal more. But since the truth was not available to my dad, I don't fault him for not giving me something he didn't fully have. What he did have was love, imagination, and an enthusiasm for life, and he gave those to me freely.

$\sim\!\sim\!\sim$

When I asked my dad to take a paternity test, he refused. Frustrated, I reached out to CeCe Moore. Although I was no longer going to appear as a guest on *Finding Your Roots*, I hoped that she could help point me in a direction toward discovery. She told me that in light of my dad's refusal, the next best option would be to do my own DNA test through all the consumer-based testing companies. If any of Earl Washington's relatives appeared in connection to my family tree, then it would mean that he was, in fact, my biological father. But if

I found myself genetically linked to another family, that would prove that I was not related to my dad and could perhaps connect me to my donor.

So, I spat in a tube and sent in my information under an alias and waited. A couple of months later Nnamdi and I sat on the couch in our living room after putting the kids to bed and opened one of my accounts to check the results.

While he logged in, I wondered if this website would become a portal into my truth. Since learning about my parents' fertility process, I'd started a deep dive into the culture of donor-born kids. The feelings I was grappling with, and had grappled with my whole life, were not unique to me. In 2019, the United Nations convened for the first time a meeting of donor-conceived and surrogacy-born people who gave speeches about their experiences and about the lack of protection for their fundamental human rights, including "the right to identity, the right to family relations, and the right not to be bought or sold in any form."

I had so many questions:

Who is my biological father?

Is he alive?

How old is he?

What is his ethnicity?

Do I have siblings?

Does he ever watch a movie and think, Huh, that person looks like me?

Do I look like him?

Do I have extended family?

How did this come to be?

How much did it cost?

What is his medical history?

What's his mental health history?

Does he struggle with addictions?

Does he have a history of depression?

Is he funny?

Is he sensitive?

Is he creative?

Does he know about me?

Does he want to?

Part of me was terrified that I would discover a sea of kids born from the same donor, transforming me from an only child to a person with twenty siblings or more. Another part longed for the feeling of connection that so many donor children write about once they meet relatives they'd never known they'd had.

Once logged in, I was excited to see names in my family tree that I didn't recognize. But as I clicked each link, they all led back to my mother. I had no paternal connections on any of the DNA websites. Not only had my donor never submitted his DNA for analysis, but not a single person on either side of his family tree had, either. On the contrary, I knew that some members of the Washington family had submitted their DNA, but none of them showed up on my tree. It would take a direct paternity test from my dad to be sure, but this meant that I was most likely not biologically related to the man who raised me.

I was fatherless.

When I approached my dad one more time about the possibility of a paternity test, initially he said he would think about it, but eventually he called me into his room, sat me down, and admitted that he simply could not weather the uncovering of any more truth.

"If you take this test, it will kill me. If you tell anyone, it will kill me," he said, almost begging.

And given his COPD, I worried that this could be true.

"I don't want you to die over this," I said, feeling myself shrinking. "I understand why you made the choices you made, but those are not my choices. I don't want to lie about who I am."

"You don't have to lie," he said, "just don't ever talk about it."

I explained to him that it comes up every single day.

"That's ridiculous," he said. "People don't talk about what sperm they came from. You don't have to think about this every day."

Without the ability to tell the truth, I was forced into a perpetual series of lies. People would tell me, "Your son looks so much like your father!" or ask, "Where are you from?" "How are your parents doing?" "Who do you look more like, your mother or your father?"

In the age of 23andMe and Ancestry.com, there are conversations about who we are and where we come from all the time. So many of my friends have been blessed with families created with the help of IVF, sperm donors, egg donors, and surrogates. But I was unable to contribute to those conversations. My silence in a room full of girlfriends talking about how they chose their sperm donors, my unwillingness to share where I came from, made me complicit in my parents' lies and mute about the miracle of my own being.

"Why's it such a big deal?" he said. And then, reaching out to me playfully, like he almost always did, he said, "I'm still betting on myself, kid. I'm taking the over-under."

I understood the joke. He wasn't really a sports-betting guy, but he had bought lottery tickets my whole life, every single day. There was an African sculpture in my parents' living room that opened like a secret vessel for valuables. Inside, it was filled with old lottery tickets, tiny papers filled with numbers that never hit. He believed in miracles and would put money on the belief that I was his.

But the gag landed on me as an unwillingness to wade through the unknowns and grapple with the truth of who I am. The picture was no longer perfect—the missing puzzle piece had been revealed. He still wanted me to fade into the painting as he had created it, to continue to be a supporting character in the story of his life. But I needed to carve a boundary. I needed to figure out how to move forward with my story regardless of how that might impact him. I needed to find a way to be OK, whether he was willing to live in truth or not.

I had to make choices that might impact my dad's emotional well-being, and that, for me, was terrifying and unimaginable. But ironically, *he* was the very person who had taught me to face the impossible and conquer my fears, and I wasn't going to stop now.

And in any case, my dad's denial was not new to me.

~~≈~~

The water is the one place where my family is always at peace, and swimming with my dad is the activity that has allowed all the friction, the judgment, the disconnect, to disappear. We love pools, we love lakes, we love beaches. We're water people.

In 2012, I took my parents on vacation to the British Virgin Islands. Although we were staying at a gorgeous resort, we rented a car one day to explore more of the island. We found a beautiful beach where a few adventurous tourists and locals were enjoying the currents on boogie boards and surfboards.

As we swam, I was taken back to a memory from when I was a kid. In our extended family we share a bizarre and rare talent for treading water. Hanging out in the lake in upstate New York and talking while moving our limbs just enough to keep our heads above the surface was something we could do, and did often, sometimes for hours at a time. When friends came to visit, they would often be amazed at our calm endurance. We began telling them that there were seats out there in the water. It was never not funny to watch a friend swimming in circles looking for a place to perch.

I love my dad very much, and I know that he loves me, but on land I sometimes struggled with how to express that love, and how to receive it. Our shared love of the water made our time together offshore more flowing, less complicated. As we dove into the Caribbean Sea and treaded water and sidestroked through the ocean that day, I noticed that we were getting farther away from the shore than I had expected. A strong undercurrent seemed to be building, so I swam to my dad and suggested that we head back. He agreed and together we flipped around, put our heads in the water, and started to swim back to shore. After about a minute, as I pushed through the growing swell, I started to feel some fatigue. When I looked over, my dad was no longer by my side.

My dad has impeccable form as a swimmer. I never asked him where he developed it—I ascribed it to a life lived as an athlete. But even as his kicks sliced through the surface and his arms arced with elegant force, he was not moving, and there were now at least ten feet between us. I felt an urgency to get back to shore, but I knew that I needed to go farther back into the ocean to help him.

I kept my head above water, breaststroking toward him while keeping him in my sights.

"Dad, you doing OK?" I shouted.

"I'm fine," he said.

Then, as I reached his side, I asked, "Hey, are you swimming as fast as you can?"

At this, he laughed, almost embarrassed, and said yes.

"OK," I said, feigning calm. But inside I was terrified.

My dad was seventy-two. The reality of my parents' aging, and my dad's recent diagnosis with COPD, had not caught up to me yet, but now they hit me with full force. As we treaded water together, he did all he could to fight the currents pulling him out deeper, while I struggled to think of a solution that could safely bring us back in. Moving myself toward the shore had required all my strength, so I knew I wouldn't be able to pull him in on my own.

I looked around and noticed two kids with boogie boards swimming about fifteen feet away. Knowing that it would be easier to pull my dad with the assistance of a flotation device, I asked him to try to stay exactly where he was, and I swam as fast as I could to ask the kids if I could borrow a board.

When I returned with their board, it was clear from the look on his face that it had taken all his strength to remain where he was. When I handed him the board, he collapsed his chest onto it with visible relief.

There were no lifeguards on this private beach, but when two surfers noticed me pulling him in on the boogie board, they paddled over to help. With their assistance, my dad was able to climb up on a surfboard and rest his whole body as they pulled him in to shore. They offered me the second board, but I declined. I wanted to feel alone, at sea, even if just for a moment. I needed to harness my power and fight through the water to affirm my strength. I had to prove to myself that despite the terror that was coursing through me, he was OK, and so was I. We were alive.

But I was also ashamed.

How could I have been so foolish? How could I have allowed us to go so far out into the ocean knowing that he was seventy-two years old and navigating a progressive respiratory illness? I knew that my dad was not someone who made decisions based on reality—he wasn't someone who would ever choose the sensible and logical over the magical and fun. He chose adventure, and I did, too. He taught me to do that. But his denial of his limitations and my willingness to be swept away in fantasy had put us in treacherous waters.

That night at dinner my dad struggled to make sense of what had happened in the ocean. He wanted to downplay the danger we had been in and seemed intent on believing that we had both been unable to swim back to shore. When confronted with the reality of how his body was changing, I saw devastation cloud his demeanor.

As I listened to him reflect on the day, I began to realize that my ability to accept and metabolize truth, just like my ability to move through the water, was perhaps stronger than his.

~~~

The devastating tragedy of the stillbirth my mother had faced had sown in me a fear that my mother's struggles in getting pregnant would or could somehow be passed on to me. There was always the voice in the back of my mind that my own journey to becoming a mother might be challenging or complicated or painful or even deadly.

Even as I got older, when the topic of the stillbirth came up, my mother was always quick to explain that she did not know why it had happened, that no one told her. And no one in her family talks about it. Neither did her doctor, nor her nurses. She doesn't even remember seeing the child. By the time she got home from the hospital, all the nursery furniture, the baby supplies, even the stroller had been whisked away to her younger sister Jeanne's house; she was then pregnant with my cousin John. There was no visual evidence of the dream that had become a nightmare; everyone was meant to just soldier on in secret as though nothing horrible had happened.

So much of our reproductive journey is cloaked in secrecy and shadows. Until I had my own devastating miscarriage and shared about it with friends, I had no idea how many women have weathered that same loss and long to talk about it, but don't. I have the same experience every time I share my abortion story with someone. It's true: We are as sick as our secrets, and there is healing in community.

When I was born, my mother's office once again became a nursery, and this time her baby was full of life. But there was a new secret to bury in that room, and she hid it masterfully. She kept it from her mother, her sisters, her best friend, and even her husband. She allowed him to abjure reality in order to protect him from it, just like she tried to protect me.

~~~

When my kids go to bed at night, before I leave the room, I almost always say, "Thank you for choosing me." This phrase came to me when I was reading a book called *The Conscious Parent* by Shefali Tsabary. In her book, Tsabary argues that we have traditionally gotten a key element of parenting backward. We have been taught to think that kids come into the world and it is our job to mold them, guide them, and help turn them into the people they're meant to be. Tsabary believes that our job is not to make our children better; rather, our children are opportunities for us to become better, to serve them, and to make room for who they are meant to be.

The idea resonated with me because it reminded me of one of my favorite Buddhist teachings. I was once at a meditation retreat with Pema Chödrön, an ordained Buddhist nun, where she told the parable of two friends sitting together before their souls incarnated and arrived on Earth. In the story, one soul turns to the other and says, "I want you to grow. I love you so much that I will choose to be your biggest teacher in this lifetime. In our lives together, I will cause you great pain and suffering and our relationship will teach you to move closer to the Divine."

As our children challenge us, if we remain committed to serving their highest good, I believe they move us closer to our best selves. Even before I was pregnant with Isabelle, I knew it was true of my relationship with Anaiya—knowing her and loving her has always made me better.

I believe that projects choose me, too. They come into my life to teach me something. They are opportunities to learn and grow. The challenges I face in playing a character and navigating the circumstances of their world are opportunities for me to be better, so that those characters can be who they're meant to be. Some lessons are clear in the moment and others only become evident long after the fact.

What is clear to me now is that I chose my dad. I didn't choose my donor as the man to raise me; I didn't choose his family. I chose my mom and dad; I chose this life, and these lessons. Even though at times it's been painful, I can now see the beauty in all of it. This life and these parents have made me exactly who I am.

And I would not change a thing.

CHAPTER FOURTEEN

CUES

The universe had been trying to tell me all along.

Three months before the revelation, I had written the following notes in the margins of the script for *Scandal*'s final episode:

> There is no room for the truth...I have to deny my truth in service to greater institution/family...What will be exposed if I step fully into my power? What is the repetitive theme of father holding truth/power over O[livia] P[ope]? Father father father...What is struggle w./father?

Looking back, I see that the cues were everywhere: There was, of course, *She Hate Me,* a film in which my character conceived a child with donor sperm from an ex-boyfriend. But there were other films, too, more stories that centered on the challenges surrounding fertility and the nontraditional ways in which people become parents. In 2009, I was approached by Rodrigo García to costar in *Mother and Child,* a movie in which I played a woman who is desperate to have a child but can't conceive. One of the most heart-wrenching scenes I've ever had to perform was when my character, Lucy, who had been promised a child via adoption, goes to the hospital to visit her newborn and finds that the biological mother has changed her mind and wants to keep the child that Lucy thought was hers.

The following year I was offered a role in a film adaptation of Ntozake Shange's seminal play *For Colored Girls Who Have Considered Suicide/When the Rainbow Is Enuf.* Tyler Perry's adaptation featured a mind-blowing assembly of actors, including some of my greatest heroes like Phylicia Rashad, Loretta Devine, Whoopi Goldberg, and Janet Jackson, as well as peers and creative sisters Macy Gray, Anika Noni Rose, Thandiwe Newton, and even a young Tessa Thompson.

But despite the material, the opportunity to work with Tyler, and the cast, accepting the role wasn't a straightforward decision. Tyler had wanted me to play the lady in blue ("Kelly" in the film). He had written Kelly's arc to be defined by her struggles with infertility, partly because a close friend of his was going through this at the time. My heart sank. I was terrified to play another woman who was chasing motherhood but devastatingly unable to conceive.

At the time I was just out of a long-term relationship. My mother, concerned, said, "If you want a child, you need to think about this. You're not getting any younger." This further cemented a fear that her struggles with infertility could become my own. Not yet knowing my dad's role in their fertility struggles, I wondered if she had passed on to me some faulty, inhospitable code. I could feel her fear for me in the question, a fear seemingly rooted in the heartbreak of giving birth to a lifeless child, and the subsequent pain of five long years of trying and failing. I didn't want to take on another role that could invite her pain into my body.

So, I said no to Tyler, but thankfully, he called back and worked on convincing me. He told me how many women were struggling with infertility like Kelly, and what a profound impact the storyline could have. He reminded me that though I had portrayed similar themes in *Mother and Child*, that was an art-house independent film. Tyler's film would have a significantly different audience—a mass audience, who would be mostly African American, and who would be willing to tread through the difficult themes he'd be presenting because of the loyalty and trust that he had built with them through the years.

So, I agreed. Filming began while I was still appearing in *Race* on Broadway. But while most of the film was shot in Atlanta, the first two weeks included exterior shots in Harlem—I began my life as Kelly shooting once again in my hometown.

And in New York there were even more cues from the universe.

Because I was living in Los Angeles when I was cast in David Mamet's play, I quickly had to find a short-term rental not too far from the Barrymore Theater. Combing through the various real estate sections of newspapers and websites,

I stumbled upon a furnished rental on Fifty-Second Street between First Avenue and the East River. This quiet cul-de-sac sits nestled between Sutton Place and Beekman Place, and looks out toward the iconic Pepsi-Cola sign on the edge of Long Island City in Queens. I fell in love with the apartment and the neighborhood surrounding it immediately. From Ze Café, the quaint breakfast nook on the corner—where Nnamdi and I met one morning in the midst of a snowstorm to have our first date over pancakes and green tea—to the local florist, the cheese shop, and the butcher, my dog (my beloved, impossibly adorable Josie B, named for Josephine Baker) and I instantly felt at home. Across the street from Ze Café was a famous French restaurant, Le Perigord (both Le Perigord and Ze Café are now gone), and next to that, unbeknownst to me at the time, sat the offices of my mother's former ob-gyn—the offices in which I was conceived decades before.

~~~

Toward the beginning of the final season of *Scandal,* my friend Reese Witherspoon sent me a book.

"I think I found something for us," she said. "Read it and let me know what you think."

That book was Celeste Ng's *Little Fires Everywhere.* It was the latest pick for Reese's Book Club, and the next limited series that she wanted to produce as a follow-up to her massively successful adaptation of *Big Little Lies.*

When I read the novel, I was immediately on board. In the series I play Mia Warren, a woman who agrees to be a surrogate for a couple who are unable to conceive (yes, I know, *again*). Agreeing to be artificially inseminated with the husband's sperm, she offers them both her egg and her womb to create a child on their behalf. But when Mia changes her mind and decides to keep their unborn child, she goes on the run, hoping to remain hidden from the man whose sperm cocreated the daughter she's raising.

When I agreed to do the series, I had no idea how much Mia Warren's story with her daughter, Pearl, mirrored my own journey with my parents. But by the time filming began almost a year and a half later, and a few months after the revelation, the parallels were obvious.

There is a confrontation scene in *Little Fires* in which Pearl questions who her father is and where she comes from. Mia insists that it doesn't matter, that she doesn't need to know. In the playing of this scene, I was gifted an opportunity to step into my parents' shoes and empathize with their need to protect the secrets of their past and their desire to shield their daughter from complicated truths. And in acting across from Lexi Underwood, who played Pearl, I got to witness myself filled with a hunger to know more of my truth. I was Pearl, named for a gem born from the agitation of the ocean.

Later in the series, Mia calls her old friend, Anita (played by Sarita Choudhury), and confides to her that Pearl has been asking a lot of questions about her father. Anita insists that I must tell her.

"But I can't," I say, echoing my own parents' fear of losing me by telling the truth.

When I got the edit of that phone call scene, I knew there was a version of my performance that was much more emotionally vulnerable. I remembered it viscerally because it was the moment on set when I surrendered my heart to my dad and felt the distress of his truth rather than mine. It was a privilege to honor how difficult the revelation had been for him, to hold space and embody his experience on-screen.

But that version hadn't made it into the edit—for some reason, they'd chosen a calmer take.

When I called our brilliant showrunner, Liz Tigelaar, she didn't think we had a more emotional version, but I guaranteed that we did. I knew it because I had lived through it. Unlike the Kerry of the past, who didn't trust her instincts, something had shifted in me since that conversation in the apartment. I now understood why I had struggled with trusting myself for all those years: my pathway from intuition to knowing had been fractured. But now I knew that I had been right in my belief; there was a deeper connection missing between my parents and me. That knowledge granted me new confidence in my capacity to trust and assert myself.

Our producing team sent me two versions of the scene and argued that the calmer one was better.

I'm not always the greatest judge of my own performances, but I now knew, more than ever, what truth felt like in my body, and I knew what it looked like on-screen. I was channeling my dad's truth through Mia, so I fought to change the edit despite the pushback. It's one of the moments I'm most proud of in *Little Fires Everywhere*. Not because of what I was able to create as an actor but because of the truth I was able to convey and then fight for my dad's truth.

~~~

These characters, these projects, had chosen me just as my children had. They were opportunities to move closer to myself, not some version of me born out of perfectionism and people-pleasing and being the good girl, but a version rooted in authenticity and the courage to be my true self, even as I grappled with knowing less about where that true self came from.

And if my kids had chosen me, then it was also true that I had chosen my parents. I came into this life choosing the unique and particular arrangement of our family of three. I wasn't born into the life of my sperm donor; I had chosen 630 Pugsley Avenue in the Bronx, apartment 12D, as in "Dad." And regardless of whether my dad's blood runs through my veins or not, I am of him. He is my dad.

Blood may be thicker than water, but love is thicker than blood.

~~~

In the spring of 2021, my mother and I did a photo shoot together for a jewelry collection I'd designed with Aurate called "The Birth of Mother." Because the collection had been inspired by elements from the ocean (shells and pearls), we headed to the beach in Malibu for the shoot.

It was an extraordinarily beautiful day. My mother was more confident in front of the camera than she had been in the past, and I was filled with pride for the collection and for our relationship—we were closer than we'd ever been. Unlike previous photo shoots we'd done, this one was happening postrevelation, so there was a new level of intimacy between us, and our photographer captured it. We held hands, we hugged, and we gazed into each other's eyes—we were like a mother-daughter version of newlyweds.

I thought about a morning six years earlier, about a week after Isabelle was born. We were hiding out in the safety of our home in Manhattan Beach, sitting on the top floor looking out over the Pacific. Nnamdi had made an office for himself in one corner of the open floor plan, and across the room was a small sectional where I often sat and nursed our newborn. That morning, when she was done feeding, I held her tiny body in my hands and looked down into her beautiful brown eyes, and I began to silently weep. There was no veil between my daughter and me; no secrets, no distance. I didn't yet know the reason for my mother's withholding, but *this* feeling—this seemingly endless loop of uninhibited love being poured back and forth from my child's eyes to mine—was new to me. I'd never quite experienced it with my own mother.

After the revelation, that all changed. My mother's eyes opened to me, and mine to her.

The jewelry collection was meant to "embody the essence of motherhood," and for my mother and me, there were no longer any secrets about her journey into motherhood—at least not with me. She was done hiding.

During the few previous shoots I'd done with my mother, I had always been more focused on the images. That day in Malibu, however, I was focused entirely on her. The depth of our new relationship was palpable, even to others. Law Roach, who styled my mother and me for the shoot, said that he was so moved when we looked at each other that he wanted to cry.

"You look so beautiful!" I said to her.

"I feel beautiful," she said, beaming.

We held each other in the sunlight and ocean breeze and sat poised on the large rocks at the edge of the water as the surf crashed at our feet and drenched the hems of our linen day dresses. While the crew dashed around trying to protect their shoes and equipment from the lapping waves, my mother and I sat by the sea, our family's sacred place, unafraid of the water.

~~~

I used to think my mother was afraid. Afraid to leave my dad, afraid to live a bold life of adventure, afraid to write and publish, afraid to feel. But it turns out she was an intrepid adventurer, bold and brave, willing to be innovative and experimental in her quest for a child.

So, it should not have been a surprise when I watched her walk herself back from the brink of death one tiny step at a time.

In April 2021, about a week after the shoot in Malibu, my mother went to get a routine colonoscopy. The prep had made her violently ill for days, and then she got a fever, which was a clear indication that something was seriously wrong.

At the emergency room, the MRI of her midsection revealed some kind of growth or blockage in her lower abdomen. She was prescribed antibiotics and fluids and was told to rest at home ahead of an appointment with a specialist. But the next day her condition worsened, so we went back to the ER, where she was admitted to the hospital.

While filling out paperwork, my mother was asked about her cancer history, and she listed three instances. I was confused—I knew about the first two: breast cancer in 2004, during the making of *Ray,* for which she'd undergone surgery and radiation; and then a tiny recurrence in 2020, during the early months of the pandemic, which required additional surgery. But this third instance was news to me. When the nurse asked for more details, my parents avoided eye contact with me and wouldn't call it cancer—my mother just kept describing "a resection."

Once again, I felt like I was underwater. What were these new truths unfolding? It just didn't add up. But I didn't ask for clarity in the moment—the immediate need was to address her pain.

The team of doctors—which included oncologists specializing in colon and reproductive health, as well as GI specialists and my own ob-gyn, Michele Hakakha—said that they needed to perform investigative surgery because the imaging was not conclusive. Despite my mask and a hat, during an earlier visit to the waiting room I had been recognized and was asked for a selfie; so during the surgery itself, I sat on a ledge in the hallway outside the waiting room, staring at my phone, the art that hung on the walls, the vending machines, and then back at my phone.

Eventually, Michele called me.

"I'm so sorry, Kerry," she said. And then, a deep breath, and too long of a pause. "There's cancer everywhere." This was the fourth time my mother was diagnosed with cancer. In 2004, I had been denied information until well after her treatment had ended; for her second diagnosis—which turned out to be colon cancer—I had not been told at all. In 2020, after the revelation, I was told within weeks of her diagnosis, but was unable to be by her side due to rigid COVID restrictions.

But this time I knew before she did.

One of the reasons why I love Michele is that she is straightforward and blunt. She is not unkind, but her desire to convey truth outweighs her need to sugarcoat.

"This is what we were afraid of," Michele said. "It has metastasized. It's not in one place; it's like sprinkles on ice cream. And it's all over."

When they wheeled her into the recovery room, I sat with my mother, waiting for her to come to. As she opened her eyes, I adjusted the bed, allowing her to sit up a bit, and asked if she wanted a sip of water. She smiled at me and silently mouthed, "Yes."

Now it was my turn to tell her difficult truths. I wanted to deliver the news with as much love as I could, but I also didn't want to stall in search of a perfect moment of comfort. I could tell she was still groggy, and I knew I'd have to tell her again, but I couldn't bear to be in the room with secrets between us.

"It's cancer," I said.

"I know..."

Her response didn't make any literal sense, as she'd been under since the surgery, but I believed her.

"Do you want to rest some more?" I said.

She nodded.

So, I stroked her arm and told her I was going to go for a walk, feeling like we both needed some time and space to process the news. As I was walking out the door she said, "Don't tell the boogeyman."

I promised her I wouldn't, wondering who her boogeyman was and what secret of hers I was supposed to keep from him. When I got back to the room, she was much more awake—I hugged her and kissed the top of her head.

"Before I left, you told me not to tell the boogeyman," I said.

She laughed. "I did?"

I sat on the edge of her bed.

"Yes," I said. "Do you remember what I told you?"

Her eyes were so tired, filled with clarity and sadness.

"I do," she said. "It's cancer."

"We don't know what kind yet—we won't know for a few days. That will dictate the doctors' thoughts around treatment. But I want you to know that we will do whatever you want to do. I will fight this with you as much as you want to fight it, but I'll also respect your wishes."

I wanted to give her permission to do what was right for her and not feel that she had to please anybody. She sat there, staring ahead, nodding pensively.

"And I'm here for you, Mom, if you want to cry or scream," I said. "I'm here for whatever you're feeling—"

"I want to fight this," she said, cutting me off.

We sat in a comfortable silence, gazing deeply into each other's eyes. Eventually she said, "I'm so glad you're here."

And then she smiled.

~~~

There would be two battles waged at Cedars-Sinai Medical Center: one, the repair and healing of the colon; and two, the war against the cancer itself. With regards to the first, my mother and I were thrust into the aggressive intimacy of bodily functions. I was suddenly wiping pee from her leg, poop from her sheets, and replacing her bedpans. I lay in the bed with her, sat by her side, knelt next to her in her tiny hospital bathroom, and held her hand in the shower. Due to COVID-19 restrictions, she was allowed only one visitor at a time—my dad would come to care for her while I occasionally took a break. But I was assigned the role of primary caretaker. My mother and I were sharing a deep presence with each other, a closeness that we both knew would not have been possible before the revelation.

For the cancer, our main weapon was chemotherapy. Just as it was about to begin, I was scheduled to depart for Northern Ireland to begin a two-week quarantine for a Netflix film called

The School for Good and Evil. With every day I spent at Cedars, my willingness to leave my mother receded. Eventually, I asked Netflix to recast my role in the film, even going as far as to check the availability of actor friends of mine. Instead, production petitioned the government of Northern Ireland to let me conduct my COVID quarantine in the United States. I had to make a legal commitment to limit my movements to either be at home or at Cedars—which had become my second home in any case—and to test regularly.

I was at Cedars primarily as a loving daughter, but I also discovered two new roles for myself: patient advocate and unofficial physician's assistant. There were two lead surgeons—a colon oncologist and a reproductive oncologist—and both remarked they'd never seen a family member (at least one who hadn't gone to medical school) absorb information the way I had. I told them that it was what I do for a living—I take information and turn it into a life.

In those weeks at Cedars with my mother, my whole world, every minute of every day, was about her care. When I could, I went home to see Nnamdi and the kids and eat with them, or tuck the children into bed, but then I'd head right back to the hospital.

Two days before I was due to board a plane to Belfast, I still wasn't sure I would be able to leave. The testing of the biopsies had not been completed—we still didn't know what kind of cancer it was, or what the exact course of treatment would be. I couldn't imagine leaving my mother with so much still unknown.

The definitive results finally came back with a few hours to spare: it was ovarian cancer, and she would need at least eight rounds of chemo.

Once the diagnosis had been delivered, I didn't know what to do. An entire film crew was waiting for me six thousand miles away, but I wanted to stay by her side. And if she needed me or wanted me to stay, my priorities were clear.

"Mom," I said, desperately wanting her to make the choice for me.

"We need to discuss Belfast," she said sternly.

I hadn't heard that kind of steel in her voice for weeks.

"I want you to go," she said.

"You do?" I said. "But chemo—"

"Yes. You'll be with me tomorrow for the first round. My sister will be here." I had arranged for Daph, who was a retired RN, to visit and help with her care. "Your dad will be here. You have delayed your departure as long as humanly possible. Now it's time for you to go."

"Why?" I said, wanting to make sure that she was being honest with me about this decision.

"Because if you stay here, that would say to me that you don't think I'm going to get better. You will just miss two rounds of chemo. We have to believe that it will work, and that you'll go do your movie and then be with me for plenty more chemo to follow."

That was my cue. I left late that night.

~~~

I never cried at Cedars—not when I got the call that there was cancer everywhere, not as I walked the empty halls of the eighth floor in the middle of the night when fear made it impossible to sleep, not when I sat alone in my mother's room and waited for her to return from one of her multiple surgeries. I didn't cry because there was too much to do, too many questions to ask and updates to share and needs of hers to attend to. But I also didn't cry because it felt so good to be with her. We were two women in a room without a veil, nothing between us.

In Northern Ireland I had rented a beautiful seventeenth-century home just a short walk from Belfast Lough, where on a clear day, you could see Scotland from the kitchen window.

On my first night, as I walked through the house alone, the rich tones of the sunset were reflected across the bay, and I thought about all the lakes and oceans and pools that we enjoyed as a family. And I thought about my mother in that hospital room. I felt the ache of her absence and I sat on the floor in the kitchen and sobbed.

As my mother tells it, I was a very independent child. Whether it was my first day of preschool, sleepaway camp, or freshman year of college, I was never timid about being away from home or separated from her. Sitting on the floor alone in that beautiful old house was the first time in my life that I remember missing my mother. I missed her because I'd been by her side in deeply intimate ways for weeks. I missed the incessant beeping of her hospital monitors, and the slow gurgle of her breathing. I missed the fine wisps of white hair matted against her scalp and the warmth in her eyes from across the room. I missed my mommy. I desperately wanted to get back to her, and I was terrified that if the chemo didn't work, I might not be able to be with her much longer.

After the first round of chemo, my mother had to remain in the hospital because a stent that had been placed in her colon had ruptured. Fixing it would require a third surgery in as many weeks, as well as the installation of an ostomy bag and a nutrition line.

I barely slept in Northern Ireland. Once my kids joined me in Belfast, they were on a sleep schedule that involved a bedtime at roughly midnight because I wanted to maintain some consistency with their virtual schooling. I had nightly conference calls with Nnamdi and my mother's medical team at about 2 a.m. (which aligned with the end of their working day in Los Angeles), reported the details of these calls to my dad and Aunt Daph, and was then up at 4:30 for a 5 a.m. call time to the set of *The School for Good and Evil.*

In between, my days were filled with the whiplash transitions between the fantastical world of the film and the daily tasks of caring for my mother from afar. I prayed that she would return home soon—despite the debilitating impacts of chemotherapy as she struggled to recover—and I focused on transforming her home into an environment where she could heal. This meant hiring nursing aides, purchasing medical equipment like a hospital bed and bedpans, a wheelchair, a walker, and a seemingly endless supply of gauze, medical tape, and gloves.

During her time at the hospital, many of her muscles had atrophied—including the muscles in her legs that helped her stand and walk, and the muscles in her throat that helped her swallow. My mother would tell me that when she tried to eat, she felt like she was gagging.

Eventually, while I was still in Belfast, she was sent home, but she was starting to waste away both physically and emotionally. When I finally came home, she was almost unrecognizable to me — she had lost more than fifty pounds. My mother had gone from being a woman just entering her eighties whom everyone assumed was a decade younger, to someone who appeared to be more than a decade older. She was exhausted, understandably so, as was her will.

I could tell I was losing her, and I was terrified; but I was grateful we'd had the conversation early on in the hospital when she told me she wanted to fight, because now I felt I had permission to help her do so, even when she felt like she couldn't.

Our first battle was reteaching my mother how to eat. Every attempt to swallow caused her to panic. She was convinced that there was a blockage in her throat, but with the help of a speech therapist, we were able to convince her that it was safe to eat to nourish herself, and as she became comfortable with solid food again, she started to come back to life.

One of the biggest frustrations we dealt with was her ostomy bag. Although we knew that it was a necessary adjustment while her colon healed, it was cumbersome and rarely stayed in place. Daph called the bag "the Pest," but I wanted to give it a gentler name, thereby giving it some dignity — and adding some levity to the moment — so I renamed it "Patsy."

I'd always been bothered by my dad's attempts to find humor in any situation, but here I was, utilizing his tools — the Patsy gag worked. The bag went from being an albatross to causing shared moments of tender kindness and comedy. There was no denying the value of this gift, the magic of laughter that my dad had given me.

Months later, when my mother's colon was repaired and the bag removed, it took a long time for the gaping hole in her abdomen to heal (chemo slowed the process down). We'd have to agitate the wound to help trigger its healing. To do so, we'd stuff it with gauze and change it twice a day. Once again, as with "Patsy," I fell back on the tools my dad had taught me and made a performance out of removing it. I'd snap my latex gloves on, show everyone that I had nothing hiding in my hands, and, like a wizard's apprentice, I would grab the end of the gauze peeking from her belly, and start to tug. It would flow and flow like a magician's rainbow scarves.

"Your belly's like a clown car, Mom!" I'd say. "Is there a rabbit in there, too?" And my parents would laugh.

I was the magician now. They had taught me their tricks. I had humor, and intelligence, and courage, and a belief in miracles at my fingertips. I was no longer a guest onstage, an audience member participating in their act. It was now my mother who had been cut in half and I was putting her back together. I stood at the center of our magic, cloaked in truth — and in the reality of blood and shit and gauze and laughter — and I conjured our healing, with my father as my apprentice. The progression of his COPD had released him from the excesses of smoking and drinking. As they approached their forty-ninth year of marriage, I witnessed in him a renewed commitment to be a more steadfast and loving partner.

One year later, for their fiftieth anniversary, I hired a professional magician to perform a private show for our family to celebrate the miracle of her recovery and their five decades together. At one point the magician asked my father for a one-hundred-dollar bill and made him write his name on it. Then he passed around an unsliced kiwi and eventually cut it open and pulled the wet banknote from it. I screamed in disbelief; my kids leapt up from the couch; my mother gasped; but my father just smiled knowingly and applauded.

There was no denying that the magic was real.

~~~

It had taken a long time to convince him, but one of the greatest gifts my dad has ever given to me came a couple of years earlier when he finally relented and agreed to a DNA test. Through a combination of family therapy sessions, his own foray into individual therapy, and many late-night heart-to-hearts, my dad somehow became willing to face the truth.

I got the results in my car, windows down, driving north on the Pacific Coast Highway toward Santa Barbara. When my cell phone rang, I saw the name of our family physician and was sure that he was calling to deliver the news.

"Hey, Kerry," he said. "So, I have your results here. Is now a good time?"

I looked out over the Pacific Ocean, dotted with surfers and brown pelicans diving in to feast. There was no better time than this.

"Sure," I said, attempting to sound calmer than I felt.

"So, it says here that there is a 0.000001 percent chance that Earl Washington is your biological father."

I laughed out loud at the math. I knew that my dad would hear that infinitesimal number as proof that there was at least a chance that he could still be my father. But I heard it for what it was. This was our reality, and it was confirmation of a truth I had already known. From that first afternoon in the apartment when my mother began to detail the complications of my origin, I knew. In that moment, it was as if my instincts and sense of self were instantly stitched back together and readied for long-term healing.

Back then, the news of the possibility that I was not genetically related to my dad felt less like a loss and more like an invitation. I had always felt that there was more to our story. But with their denial that anything was amiss in the years before the revelation, they had abducted my deepest instincts. I had not been allowed to feel, or to know myself. My biology had been their enemy. Consequently, I had learned to survive without a true relationship to it. I didn't know my body; I couldn't read its signs. I didn't rest when I was tired, didn't register when I was hungry, couldn't decipher when I was full. Over time, my body became my enemy, and I couldn't bear the discomfort of being fully present in my skin. I sensed that my embodiment scared my mother and threatened my dad.

Presence itself—being fully alive and aware—became something to avoid.

The fuel that had powered our family was pretending.

~~~

I was on my way to Santa Barbara to join Nnamdi, our kids, and my parents for the weekend. Caleb had asked to go whale watching for his third birthday, and while my parents were not joining us on the boat the next day, we were all gathering that weekend to celebrate by the shore.

Since I'd gotten the news from the doctor, I'd been filled with an almost electric sense of freedom. On the drive, the ocean and the sky seemed suddenly without limits, and I felt supercharged with the power of naked truth. I no longer had anything to be afraid of. I was no longer encumbered by the story my parents had told me about who I was, no longer trapped by the need to pretend that I believed it. But as I reached the outskirts of Santa Barbara, I felt that power become tainted by my concern for how my dad would react.

When I arrived, my kids were splashing around in the ocean, so I took the opportunity to invite my parents to our room to share the results of the paternity test.

"I talked to the doctor," I said.

My dad again curled into the corner of a sofa. This time, though, he looked stoic as he braced for the news. My mother sat in an armchair next to him, and Nnamdi sat on the other end of the sofa, closer to me.

"I'm so sorry," I said to my dad. "The test results show a less than one percent chance that you and I are biologically related."

My dad took a deep breath.

"I'm not going to make a joke about the odds," he said, releasing us all from the need to pretend.

I thanked him, and I told him that I loved him. All four of us hugged, and then my dad excused himself to take a nap.

$\sim\!\sim\!\sim$

I used to have a ritual when I finished filming a project: I would take myself on vacation alone somewhere, to spend time relaxing and returning to whatever semblance of self I could muster.

Years before I was married with children, I wrapped filming on an intense independent movie called *Life Is Hot in Cracktown*. I chose Maui as my retreat. One morning, I signed up for a guided kayaking trip in the ocean, where we sat for hours waiting to hear and perhaps see the tiny burst of air that signaled the presence of a whale. When it finally happened, we noticed two blowholes within our view, and one was closer than either my guide or I had anticipated. I lifted my paddle out of the water and turned excitedly toward my guide. He kept his gaze ahead on the whales, nodded his head, and said, "Don't move."

Seconds later, a third whale—a calf—leapt out of the ocean in a show of playful exuberance and landed with a great splash maybe eight feet in front of my kayak while the first whale, an adult the size of a school bus, began to circle toward me to get a closer look at us.

My guide had already explained that these blue whales were not carnivorous creatures—they were wholly uninterested in us as prey. The only danger we faced was that we might be flipped or tossed into the ocean.

I tried to remain calm while watching the calf continue to frolic like a theatrical toddler seeking the attention of a captive audience.

"The calf's showing off," the guide said. And in response, its mother moved to pass under me. My kayak rose and stayed there as she paused and angled herself toward the surface so that her eye could meet mine.

Everything stopped. It seemed that all of life was swimming in that single eye. I watched her watching me. Her gaze was maternal, it was an offering, an evaluation, a warning, a witnessing. *Was she trying to tell me something?* I felt a deep connection, a belonging to all that is. And then she kept swimming.

There I was, surrounded by three blue whales—a male, a female, and a child—making their migration back from the warmer southern oceans.

"It's not the father," my guide explained as we paddled back to shore. My entire body was still trembling with excitement. "That male is the whale who wants to mate with the mother next season. He accompanies the mother and her child on their journey to prove himself worthy."

It was another hint, another cue: The three of them were a family forged to survive the crossing. He had chosen them; they had chosen each other.

He may not have been the biological father, but in their journey together, he was the dad.

EPILOGUE
MARISA

Marisa is my middle name and the hidden identity at the center of me.

When I was a little girl and asked my mother what "Marisa" meant, she told me, "princess of the sea," as if I were straight out of a fairy tale. She and my dad had wished upon a star.

I know now that "Marisa" means just "of the sea," and for me, it has come to represent how much I love the water, how I feel at home there, and the ways in which, as a child, I imagined myself as a mermaid or a synchronized swimmer. But also, when one is "at sea," it means they are lost, without a land to belong to, or a ship to travel in; it means one is a refugee.

"This is not something people talk about," my dad once said, referring to infertility issues. I understand what he meant. We carry so much shared collective shame and trauma around our reproductive challenges. And for men, their presumed power and masculinity is often tied to their ability to seed future generations.

In middle school, I decided that if I ever got married, I would keep the name Washington because I felt sad that my dad didn't have a son and therefore the name might end with him. I was determined not to be the cul-de-sac on Washington Street. I didn't know that there was already a finality there. My dad was the end of the road in terms of Samuel Washington's genetics, no matter what I did in the future. But beyond the genetics, I am Earl Washington's kid—it's the Washington in me that dreams and believes and performs and entertains and refuses to disappoint.

And yet, when anyone talks about being reunited with a lost relative or family member—or finds any missing puzzle piece from their past—there's a longing in me that gets stirred up, an envy, a hunger.

〜〜〜

When I got married, there wasn't enough space to have Kerry Marisa Washington Asomugha on the certificate. I wanted to add Washington as my middle name, but I didn't want to give up Marisa. So now, legally, my first name is Kerry Marisa, my surname is Asomugha, and my middle name is Washington. I will not let go of the man who raised me.

〜〜〜

Skip Gates and CeCe Moore have continued their search, but as I write this, we still have not found my donor. I think about meeting him — fantasize about it sometimes — but I'm also beginning to accept that I may never know him. And I don't need to. Or at least I don't think I do.

What I'm learning to do in my life is accept the void, let my dad who raised me be the center of his story, let my biological donor be the center of his, while I focus on being the center of my own story and seeking a deeper truth for myself.

My life is not about my donor, nor about my parents. My life is my own.

Kerry is what my mother chose.
Washington is my dad.
Asomugha is my future.
Marisa belongs to me.

〜〜〜

There is something so comforting about being under the surface of water and looking up. The sound is just a bit muffled; my vision is slightly obscured, and that muted state of reality is what life has always felt like to me. With goggles, everything in the water is hyperclear, but if I look up to the surface, I see a fun-house mirror. All the images are moving through space, like those squiggly lines from old movies and TV shows.

I have always felt in my relationship with my parents, and in life in general, that I haven't trusted what I'm looking at, never fully believing what I'm seeing. It's true for sound, too — I can still hear things while underwater, but there's a chamber of silence, of the unknown, between the world above the surface and me.

I find healing when I'm in water because the one voice I hear clearly is my own.

ACKNOWLEDGMENTS

Thank you to:

Shonda Rhimes, who told me to write a book ten years ago.

Cait Hoyt at CAA, who urged me to write a book five years ago.

Tracy Behar at Little, Brown, who acquired a book from me two years ago, even though it wasn't this one.

Reisha Perlmutter, for our gorgeous book cover.

Kathy Atkinson, for truly believing I can do anything.

My mom and dad, without whom there would have been no story to tell. I love you.

My husband and children, for giving me time and space to tell it. I love you.

Skip Gates, for the inciting incident.

My team at Simpson Street and KW Inc., for taking care of the sandbox while I played in a new one.

A special thanks to all the Gladiators and fans. I am deeply appreciate of your love and support.

And to the entire teams at Washington Square Arts; CAA; Hansen, Jacobson, Teller, Hoberman, Newman, Warren, Richman, Rush, Kaller, Gellman, Meigs & Fox, L.L.P.; the Lede Company; Spielman Koenigsberg & Parker, L.L.P.; and Little, Brown, for making this dream a reality.

VESTAVIA HILLS
LIBRARY IN THE FOREST
1221 MONTGOMERY HWY.
VESTAVIA HILLS, AL 35216
205-978-0155